ALSO BY THE SAME AUTHOR
The Imaginative Tree

FOR HUMAN BEINGS ONLY

FOR
HUMAN BEINGS
ONLY

A PRIMER OF HUMAN UNDERSTANDING

Sarah Patton Boyle

NEW YORK
1964

TO
DR. EDWIN BANCROFT HENDERSON
　　of Falls Church, Virginia,
　　pioneer in human relations,

AND TO
JUDGE J. WATIES WARING
　　formerly of Charleston, South Carolina,
　　first to rule that
　　segregation in itself is discrimination;

　　with affection, admiration, and deep respect
　　I dedicate this book, which attempts
　　to follow where they and
　　their brave wives, Mary and Elizabeth,
　　have for many decades led.

ACKNOWLEDGMENTS

I wish to express grateful indebtedness to the following persons:

Nancy Moore, of New York City, for expert editorial help that enabled me to write this book quickly.

The Rev. Henry B. Mitchell, of Trinity Episcopal Church, Charlottesville, Virginia; Dr. Coragreene Johnstone and Dr. Hobson Thompson, of Elizabeth City State Teachers College, North Carolina; Dr. E. B. Henderson of Falls Church, Virginia; and others for valuable criticisms and comments.

Ruth Haefner, of Portland, Oregon; Edith Hussey, of Falls Church, Virginia; and others for helpful suggestions.

Eugene Williams, Otelia Jackson, Pernetha Gilbert, Frances Brand, Virginia Carrington, Beatrice Fowlkes, and Jane Foster, of Charlottesville, Virginia; J. Raymond Henderson, of Los Angeles, California; Vivian Carter Mason, of Norfolk, Virginia; and Winfred Mundle, of Richmond, Virginia—for sustaining friendship and valuable promotional aid.

Acknowledgment is also due *Ebony* Magazine and *The SCLC Newsletter* for permission to print certain passages which first appeared in their pages.

CONTENTS

To the Reader   11

PART ONE: FOR WHITE ONLY   15

    Introduction   16
1 The Black Side of the Wall   17
2 A Sheet of White Paper   25
3 Getting Acquainted   33
4 Inclusion Is the Keynote   39
5 Early Days of Friendship   44
6 Watch Your Language   51
7 Typical Images   57
8 Integration Bafflement   64
9 The Haunted House   69

PART TWO: FOR COLORED ONLY   77

    Introduction   79
1 Poisoned Wounds   81
2 Why It Happened   87
3 Divergent Customs   93
4 More Stereotypes   99
5 The Gangster in the Haunted House   106
6 Bulldogs for Brotherhood   113

PART THREE: FOR ALL OF US   119

Appendix   125

TO THE READER

This is, I believe, the first book of its kind. Its purpose is to smooth the rough path to friendship between individual white and colored Americans.

Through segregation, legal and *de facto,* one-tenth of our nation's citizens have become so estranged from the other nine-tenths that misinterpretation, friction, and pain often result when members of the two groups seek to become acquainted. Yet I believe the time has come when individual friendships, more than anything else, will heal the wounds of our nation.

Books, articles, speeches, unless used as manuals for personal involvement, are almost useless in promoting understanding between us and our alienated brothers. So little communication has existed for so long that many assumptions, ideas, phrases, even many words, have entirely different implications in the two groups. The result is that in talking to an American of another color, you can say one thing but be heard as saying something entirely different.

It is, therefore, necessary to step into another dimension of communication, the language of daily fellowship. We need a Peace Corps of individuals who will scale the segregation wall from both sides with determination and dedication.

This book attempts to point out—when possible, to clear up—some of the common misunderstandings that occur between Negro and white Americans. It lays no claim to scholarship, finality, or completeness. I have simply set down a few of such insights as I have gained from fourteen years of intergroup relationships—some cherished, some sighed over.

It is a brief, simple book while the problem it deals with is long and intricate. An exhaustive study would require many thick volumes. I try here merely to focus attention on some usual sources of misunderstanding and to awaken our insight into the minds and hearts of persons of the other group. The reader's interest in creating good will and making friends across the color line is assumed. No attempt is made to convince the reluctant.

It is hoped that each individual will ponder his own situation and search his own soul, seeking to apply to his particular case the general principles and limited examples here reviewed.

I hope the book will be used by individuals seeking to initiate, broaden, or deepen friendships with persons of a different ethnic background, that the book will also be helpful to study groups, and will prove a useful source or guide for human relations workshops and intergroup discussions.

Some may object that self-consciousness between individuals will result from the book's analysis of common errors. Indeed, it will—at first. Some learning necessarily begins with self-consciousness. Wrong behavior patterns cannot be made to give way to right ones without keen awareness of the process.

Not until habitual errors have been rooted out and sound social attitudes firmly planted can we hope for natural relationships between white and Negro Americans. But even self-consciousness is better than the perpetual misconstruing and offense giving which now holds center stage in the human relations drama throughout our land.

Integration is upon us—upon those who wish it and those who do not. The task now is to make it work. This will not be easy, yet it can be done if many firm bridges of individual fellowship reach out across the canyon of misinterpretation which divides our land. This book is a guide to bridge building.

Integration can be made to work because it must. Here lies the one hope for us all. Our divisions in America are only the world's divisions in miniature. If we learn to create an indivisible nation, we can move toward creation of an indivisible world.

Surely all can now see that time has run out. Either we quickly move toward the brotherhood of all men or there will not be any men.

PART ONE:

FOR

WHITE

ONLY

INTRODUCTION

Although this book is divided into two parts, "For White Only" and "For Colored Only," it should be remembered that it is presented as a unit *For Human Beings Only*. Just as white and colored Americans are interdependent, so are the two parts of the book. Both must be read by all, and the individual chapters, as well as the parts, should be read in the order in which they are placed. Part One contains information necessary to an understanding of Part Two.

1

THE BLACK SIDE
OF THE WALL

Nineteen hundred sixty-three marked the outbreak
of an American revolution which had long been smoldering.
Negro citizens throughout the nation resorted to action that
made clear what their many words had not: that they would not,
could not, wait longer for full desegregation and equal opportunity, that no price was too high for the goals they sought.

To many whites this demand for speed and refusal to com-
promise was incomprehensible. "Can't the Negro see," they
asked in troubled voices, "that it is to his own advantage not to
push people faster than they can go in good will?"

The answer is that indeed the Negro cannot see. To him
segregation is at best a prison, at worst a torture chamber. He
is not interested in talk about the "advantages" of enduring it
longer.

The segregation wall has been not only one which colored
people could not climb over. It has also been one which white
people could not see over. Even when sympathetic to the cause
of equality, few whites have had any conception of what it is like
to be a segregated Negro. Despite the many articulate voices

recently raised on this subject, the thick barrier of ignorance still stands.

Yet until the truth is at least glimpsed, it is nearly impossible to comprehend some of the reactions we shall meet across the color line in our rapidly desegregating land. The personalities, the conduct, of Negro citizens grow out of the life that exists on the black side of the wall.

The thumbnail sketch which follows will do no more than barely suggest the conditions on that side of the wall. But my purpose, which is merely to remind readers of what they have read or heard elsewhere about this situation (they probably have read or heard a great deal or they would not be reading such a book as this), and to point out and analyze the kind of experiences which lie behind attitudes we often meet in the course of integrated activities.

Our concern will not be with the events themselves but with their effect on the persons subjected to them, and I shall not attempt to give a balanced picture or to distinguish between conditions that still exist and those of the recent past. The situation is changing fast and what is bitter fact today may be only history tomorrow; but its effect on the consciousness of its victims will remain.

Nor shall I pinpoint the region where certain happenings have occurred. Negroes move about—especially they move out of the South—carrying their conditioning with them. In any part of the United States one meets colored citizens who are the product of experiences that took place far from where they now live. It is well to note, however, that by and large the lot of the Negro everywhere has been far worse than most white people suspect.

Let us glance at five general characteristics of life when lived on the black side of the segregation wall: dangers, handicaps, inconveniences, humiliations, emotional stresses.

DANGERS

The horrors of lynching are well known, but few whites realize the devastating effect on Negroes of the mere awareness that such a thing could happen. When I began to integrate myself in 1950, no lynching had occurred in my area for many years. The likelihood of one occurring was more remote than of a Negro being struck by lightning; yet every Negro I talked with harbored an overshadowing consciousness of the *possibility* of a lynching.

The dread is kept alive by news from afar. A brutal lynching anywhere pours rage and horror into millions of colored Americans great distances away. For them it is a personal experience. Perhaps they identify with the victim because they know that had they been there, it might have happened to them or their sons, since one need not actually be guilty, but only accused, to suffer.

When the lynchers escape punishment, most whites shake their heads over the miscarriage of justice, and then forget it. Negroes smolder, taking it as an affront not only to principle but also to their very persons—and they do not forget.

But at least lynching is illegal. Injustice in courts of law in some ways is more demoralizing. What hope is there when both judge and jury act on an unconscious assumption that a Negro is *more likely* to be guilty than a white?

In regard to rape especially, the cut of discrimination has been deep, the assumption often being that rape is more a calamity to white than to colored women. In many places the maximum penalty for a white raping a Negro has been unheard of, whereas Negroes accused of raping whites have often received the death sentence. At any trial credence is more commonly given to white than to Negro testimony, and countless injustices have been the inevitable result.

In the summer of 1963 a young clergyman told me of

receiving telephone calls threatening his life because of his integration efforts. He tensely rejected my suggestion that he appeal to the police. The grounds for his decision were that since he was a Negro, law enforcement officers might sympathize with and join his persecutors.

Obviously, he feared police brutality more than he feared the unknown terrorists who were tormenting him. My stomach felt queasy as I realized that here in our "land of liberty" fellow Americans feel no safer than we would feel traveling in an enemy country in time of war.

Note that for all my long-familiar knowledge of injustice across the color line, it took a *personal experience with a friend* to bring this truth home. In fellowship with others we identify with their emotions and our eyes begin to see their worlds.

OTHER DANGERS

Negroes are also much aware of a different kind of danger that segregation brings. Insurance statistics show more ill-health and a higher death rate among them than among whites. These conditions stem from their unequal economic opportunities, which spelled out simply mean inferior sanitation, housing, clothing, diet, and medical care. But there is another less frequent, yet more shocking, factor in these statistics.

Many hospitals have followed a policy of assigning one floor or one ward to Negro use. When these specific facilities are full, colored patients are automatically refused admission, even in emergencies. I cannot forget the eyes of a young wife whose husband, refused admission at a nearby hospital, died on his way to a distant one; or those of the man crippled for life because he did not receive attention in time. In both cases they said that there were vacant beds in the white part of those hospitals at the very time admission was refused.

There is also the ever present danger of unemployment.

North and South, loss of livelihood is always just around the corner for persons who know they are always the last to be hired, the first fired whenever jobs are scarce.

HANDICAPS

The handicaps of segregation may stem chiefly from poor educational and job opportunities. But from thence they are reflected in nearly every area of the Negro's life: his incentive, self-respect, confidence, health, energy—indeed his whole apparatus for achievement and self-fulfillment.

Even where all-Negro schools do not fall short of white schools in facilities, curriculum or both, they cannot prepare colored children for life in a nation that is nine-tenths white. Segregated white schools, on the other hand, propagate discrimination. Persons who experience, during their formative years, no relationships of equality with colored children are not likely later to give equal chances to colored adults in any walk of life.

Negroes know that a segregated school, white or Negro, retards democratic life in a biracial nation. Indignation against those who insist on maintaining such schools is inevitable on the part of individuals who have been made to suffer because of these segregated schools.

An insurmountable handicap in finding suitable employment, segregation—legal or *de facto*—has often meant that Negroes lack commonplace opportunities that whites take for granted—clerking in a store, working in a mill, typing in an office.

In many areas it has been impossible for a Negro, regardless of ability or degree of preparation, to rise above the day laborer class. Throughout the nation colored citizens have had to expend twice as much natural ability, energy, and concentrated effort to achieve the same degree of success as a white. Often a step above the lowest rung has been impossible, even for the most gifted.

INCONVENIENCES

The hourly inconvenience of being colored is unimaginable to persons who have not experienced it. "I was with a colored friend at lunchtime yesterday," a woman told me, "and we had to walk fifteen blocks to find a place that would serve us. I got my first glimpse of what discrimination means in everyday living."

One reason why it is vital that we make friends across the color line is that it takes personal experience really to awaken most of us. Secondhand information seldom brings us this understanding.

We all know about "white-only" rest rooms. But unless we have colored friends few of us know that often no toilets at all have been provided for Negroes. In huge areas of many towns all toilets have been "white-only." Unspeakable discomforts and embarrassments have resulted.

When motoring, lodging has often been an enormous problem, precious hours being wasted simply in seeking a place to sleep. Often none can be found and the Negro has to drive on, although too weary to drive safely, or else sleep, uncomfortable and apprehensive, in his car.

In many towns Negroes have been permitted neither to try on wearing apparel in stores, nor to return a garment if, on arriving home, it is found not to fit. This rule, remember, has been applied to a people who, by and large, can less afford such financial losses than can whites. Often, too, it is customary to wait on whites first, even when colored customers are there first.

HUMILIATIONS

All these situations are occasions for humiliation as well as being dangers, handicaps, or inconveniences, for they all imply that to be colored is to be unacceptable. But other humiliations have been added. Small distinctions, too numerous to name, have been practiced regularly between white and Negro Americans. Signs proclaiming WHITE ONLY, COLORED ONLY, NEGROES IN THE REAR, have been hourly reminders that Negro Americans were considered unfit to share facilities with white. And even the simple courtesy titles—Mr., Mrs., and Miss—have often been denied colored citizens in personal conversations, in newspapers, and on the air.

EMOTIONAL STRESSES

The greatest temptation to hate white Americans, however, lies less in the many trials listed above than in the inner destruction which often comes to gifted young Negroes when their true situation dawns on them. This has been and is a nightmare for colored parents. Each knows that despite all efforts to stave off facing it, an honest answer has to be given one day to the eternal question, "Why can't I go there?"

Evade it as he will, the parent must finally reply, "Because *you are colored.*" He then has to watch creeping upon his child the terrible realization that to be colored is an inescapable badge of disgrace in the land which is his home.

There is no way to prevent this realization coming to the colored child in a society that operates on the assumption that the best is for whites and that the admission of a Negro to white preserves somehow lowers standards. There is no way out. Driven by love and fear, Negro parents have, over the years, tried everything.

Nor has any parent been able to predict how his child will react to this realization. Some young people have simply lost motivation, their incentive withering on the stem. Bright ambitions, suddenly seeming hopeless, were abandoned, and lethargy settled in. Other young people fiercely lit faggots of hatred that will flicker until the damp grave puts them out. Still others, angry-eyed, have turned to the quick redress offered by crime.

Hardly less heart-rending to watch have been the struggles of the young who fought back with their highest and best, yet could not win against the fate of being a segregated Negro in a nation that is 90 per cent white. A few, a handful, have triumphed in spite of everything—a few among the thousands who might have triumphed had they had an equal chance.

Suppose our own children faced such ordeals, such odds against achievement and fulfillment. What would we do, what would we *not* do, to bring true for them the promise of our land, the promise which every school day colored children repeat: one nation indivisible with freedom and justice for *all!*

This sketch is of the black side of the wall when it was harder to climb than, I hope, it soon shall be. Things are getting better. But the mark of what was will remain. For if all discrimination were to be wiped, like tears, from the face of our nation, it could not be wiped from the hearts of 20 million Americans. *

* For a picture in depth of the black side of the wall I suggest you read *Black Like Me* by John Howard Griffin; *Black Boy* by Richard Wright; *Notes of a Native Son* and *Nobody Knows My Name*, both by James Baldwin.

2
A SHEET OF
WHITE PAPER

"Why can't our two races get along together?" a blue eyed, sandy haired college student earnestly asked another student. "Just because I belong to one race and you to another race, are we different inside? If individuals can be friends, so can races. I don't understand all this racial strife. To me, one race is just like another."

Silence.

"What's the matter? Don't you agree that your race and mine should get on?"

"I agree."

"Then why won't members of your race talk to me? I always get the deep freeze—like now."

"You really want to know?"

"Yes, I do. I'm getting fed up. I try for interracial friendship and get nowhere."

The other student studied the ground for a moment, then opened his brief case, removed a sheet of white paper and silently extended it.

His companion looked startled. "I don't get it. You mean I act lily white? I *try* not to."

"Read the watermark. Think about it awhile. If you don't get the point, ask me after class." He walked away.

The white boy held the paper up to the light and read the watermark: RACERASE.

Telling about it later, he said that the mark jumped out at him as one combination of words, then another. First he read "Race! Race!" and saw in a flash that his harping on the subject created the very barrier he wanted removed. Later he read "Race erase!" and grasped the fact that the concept of race is an abstraction fit only for academic uses, that in personal relationships it is artificial, misleading, offensive, and should be *erased* from one's thinking.

It is wryly amusing that while he successfully got the deep implications from his lesson, he failed to note, indeed he had to be told later about, his irritating habit of using the word *race* or *racial* so often that in a one-minute conversation he was guilty of using it nine times.

THE WORD "RACE"

Until a few decades ago most white Americans believed in the existence of "racial differences" in character and intelligence that would stand forever as granite-like obstacles to shared activities and mutual understanding. Some still do.

During the rise of Naziism a rash of books by respected German scientists appeared in support of the "master race" theory. They still are quoted by zealous segregationists. But reputable modern scientists—biologists, sociologists, psychologists, anthropologists—now combine voices in rejecting the assumption that such a thing as innate racial superiority exists.

Anthropology, of course, is "the study of races, physical and mental characteristics, distribution, customs, social relationships." (*Webster's New World Dictionary*) On anything concerning race, anthropologists are the final experts; they draw on and evaluate relevant findings of all other scientists. Their conclusions on this subject are recognized as the soundest that modern science affords, and any opinion which ignores their conclusions may justly be dismissed as uninformed. It is, therefore, of great moment that the official national body of anthropologists unanimously adopted the following resolution, which they reaffirmed and released for general publication November 13, 1961:

"The American Anthropological Association repudiates statements now appearing in the United States that Negroes are biologically and in innate mental ability inferior to whites and reaffirms the fact that there is no scientifically established evidence to justify the exclusion of any race from the rights guaranteed by the Constitution of the United States. The basic principles of equality of opportunity and equality before the law are compatible with all that is known about human biology. All races possess the abilities needed to participate fully in the democratic way of life and in modern technological civilization."

The fact that, as a group of psychologists expressed it, "there is no scientifically acceptable evidence of inborn differences between racial groups in abilities," is well known to Negroes. They have been taught the fact in high school, if not before. But most whites learn it only from certain college courses —usually in anthropology or sociology—if they happen to take them.

Because Negroes have suffered many insults and handicaps as a result of popular misconceptions of race, even the word itself is offensive to many of them. It has not quite been dropped from their vocabulary, but modern colored Americans use it sparingly. A white does well to avoid it in talking with them, unless no other term will convey his meaning. This is seldom the case.

COLORED VERSUS NEGRO

A common question asked by whites who are seeking to reach across the color line is whether their newly discovered brothers prefer to be called *Negroes* or *colored people.* The answer is, "That depends on whom you are talking to."

Some passionately prefer *colored people,* others with equal passion press for *Negroes.* I know of two Negro newspapers of about the same circulation with offices less than one hundred miles apart. One so detests the word *Negro* that the editors change it to *colored,* even in direct quotations. (This has happened in quoting my speeches.) The other paper follows the reverse policy. I do not recall ever having seen the term *colored people* used on its pages.

A state president of the National Association for the Advancement of Colored People once informed me that the best procedure is to use both terms interchangeably. Following this advice for many years, I have received no complaints. Of course, once we have learned which term our listener prefers, we should try to use it exclusively when speaking with him.

OTHER WORDS

Almost everyone today, even in the South, knows that he should avoid such epithets as "pickaninny, coon, nigger, jig, and darky." But with utmost innocence one may use words that offend almost as much.

Take *boy,* for instance. You are on shaky ground if you refer to any colored male above the age of twelve as a boy, and you cannot hope to be forgiven if he is twenty-five or older. It makes no difference if you call all your son's high school and college friends "boys"; when the person is colored, you must call him "young man." It matters not at all if you consider it a mark of tact to refer to your husband's graying, paunchy friends as "the boys." You must say "men," better still, "gentlemen," when speaking of mature colored citizens.

If this makes Negroes sound stuffy, it does not reflect the truth. Their rejection of the term *boy* as applied to themselves is an inescapable reaction to the offensive Southern custom of using that word to address Negroes of any age. For example, calling out, "Hey, boy, you got a match?" to a venerable colored citizen, as though all Negroes were bellhops.

Or take the term *Negress.* Until a few decades ago even dictionaries listed it as correct. Newer ones have adopted the Negro's view of it. My own dictionary (*Webster's New World*) notes that, like Jewess, it is "often a patronizing or contemptuous term." Some smaller dictionaries omit the word. Incidentally, use of this term seems almost entirely to be a non-Southern offense. But I have heard Northerners who are wholly dedicated to the colored American's cause use it.

MISPRONUNCIATION

On the other hand, almost all white Southerners mispronounce the word *Negro.* Quite unaware of wrongdoing, they say it—as they do many other words—with such a slur that it little resembles the true phonetic rendering. To a non-Southern ear, white or black, it often sounds like *nigger,* and even those able to distinguish the difference commonly think it a deliberate attempt to approach that epithet closely without quite saying it. This, I assure you, is never the case: if a Southern white wants to say *nigger,* he says it.

What they actually are saying is *Nigra,* which they truly think is how the combination of letters N-e-g-r-o is pronounced.

With the characteristic Southern softening of the *r* toward an *ah* sound in both *Nigra* and *nigger,* it is easy to see how the non-regional ear would fail to catch the difference. Yet the Southerner's mouthing of Virginia, Carolina, and New Orleans (if he lives there) is hardly better than his rendering of "Negro"— *Vuhginyuh, C'lina,* and *Nyu Aw'ins.*

Less than a score of years ago most colored Southerners also said *Nigra,* and many still do—often correcting themselves with embarrassed laughter. Therefore, in the South—the deep South especially—even from the tongue of a white, it gives less offense than in other parts of the country. But what acceptability it has left is fast vanishing. If you are a Southern white, you simply must practice saying Knee-grow (as if it were two words) until it has a natural sound to you.

I well know that this is hard. Years after I thought I had my own Southern tongue trained to say it correctly, I learned from a friend that I was still pronouncing it only half-right. I was pronouncing it Ni-GROW.

I have recently heard Negroes complain that in the North there is an increasing tendency to mispronounce the word in another way. Northerners often say KNEE-gra—again, only half-right.

BADGES OF BROTHERHOOD

The majority of Negro leaders prefer the word *group* to *race.* When it seems too inexact for a specific purpose, *ethnic group* can be used. While this phrase may seem awkward, rewards for using it are high. It is the equivalent of a badge which says, "I believe in brotherhood." Negroes know that few whites think of discarding the word *race* until they are active in the struggle to get barriers down.

Another badgelike word is *minority.* Occasionally, instead of saying *Negroes* or *colored people,* say "members of the minority." Though cumbersome to use four words where one or two will do, it reveals to listeners that you are thinking of rights rather than of differences.

Form a habit of using words and combinations of words that imply unity rather than division. Sometimes a qualifying word accomplishes this effect. When we say simply *Negroes,* the mind's eye sees a separate segment of mankind. When we say *Negro Americans,* our hearts know that *Americans* is the important word. Saying *colored citizens,* instead of *colored people,* also has a binding-together effect. A colored person could be a foreigner, even a savage. A colored citizen is one of us.

In discarding the word *race,* of course, something similar happens. *Race relations* suggests persons miles apart being brought within speaking distance. When, instead, we use the phrase *intergroup relations,* the effect is more friendly; while if we say *human relations,* there is a feeling of inclusiveness, that all barriers are gone.

When I first heard the latter phrase given the specific meaning it now commonly carries on the civil rights front, I exclaimed, "Why, it's too confusingly vague to be of use!" Yet to date I recall no occasion when it confused anyone.

BADGES OF REJECTION

Some words and phrases are badges with an opposite message—rejection. By their use persons reluctant to accept their darker brothers can instantly be recognized. The phrase "forced integration" is one. Unless a person favors exclusion, he feels that integration is the natural state, that *forced* is therefore correctly applied only to segregation.

Another combination of words used often—and only—by segregationists is "race mixing." It is their way of describing integration in any form, from intermarriage to sharing a public auditorium.

THE WHITE MAN AT HIS WORST

But let us not imagine that only segregationist whites are painful to Negroes. The little story at the beginning of this chapter was told about a young man newly awakened to the cause of brotherhood who was visibly, and verbally, burning with zeal for "interracial friendship." To his colored companion he appeared unattractive, frightening, and insulting.

He was unattractive because of the eager-beaver ardor which often attends such an aim; such ardor, while valuable when applied to abstract causes, is distasteful when focused on oneself. He was frightening because a healthy relationship must be based on congeniality. When an ulterior motive is introduced, a sense of being more a quarry than a person results.

To be sought merely because one happens to be in a certain classification is insulting. A young man may be thrilled at fawning attentions from a pretty girl if she appears to like him personally, but angry if he sees that she is only "boy crazy." Again, I am pleased when I am approached by a person who thinks my writings helpful, annoyed if merely "collecting authors" is the person's aim.

If we wish a particular colored brother to grasp the hand we offer, it must be crystal clear that we offer it primarily, not because he is colored, but because there is something about him personally to which we feel akin.

3

GETTING ACQUAINTED

When you set out to win friends among Negroes, you will not understand the difficulties you meet unless you keep in mind what the person's experience must have been by virtue of his being a member of a segregated minority. Making friends who happen to be colored is just like making other friends—with two important exceptions. First, you must overbalance their feeling that whites want nothing to do with them. Second, you must keep their probable sore spots continually in mind.

THE PARADOX

A recurring paradox in relationships across the color line is that most Negroes think it of first importance that you forget they are colored and treat them exactly as you would a white, yet if you do precisely that, you probably will continually give offense and will not succeed in winning them as friends.

There are two main reasons for this paradox. First, few Negroes know how whites treat other whites, so that when you treat a Negro just as you would a white friend, this is the very time when he probably thinks you are not doing it. Second, few Negroes are aware of the extent of their own sensitivity, of how easily they conclude that they are being snubbed, ignored, laughed at, or rejected.

True, there is as much variation in the attitudes of Negroes toward whites as of whites toward Negroes. Some colored Americans are spontaneously responsive to friendliness, others shy, withdrawn, suspicious, or hostile. You must play each opportunity by ear. But, in general, when you set out to treat Negroes just as you would whites, you must add, "That is, whites who have had many bitter experiences which incline them to doubt the sincerity and good will of strangers."

Please keep in mind that here I am speaking always of *acquaintances, not friends.* Once a friendship is established on a firm footing, naturally no rules can apply and none should be sought.

When dealing with strangers or with acquaintances who are not yet friends, we all follow, whether we are aware of it or not, the rules of behavior which we have been taught are polite and correct. But when we cross the color line, we soon learn that the old rules of behavior that are second nature with us do not produce the same results they do within our own group. We have to learn a whole new keyboard of courtesy and tact.

Of course, all relationships must be played more by ear than by note, and no specific rule is useful. But a good over-all rule to follow with colored strangers and acquaintances is to behave toward them somewhat as you would with a shy but honored guest in your home—that is, with all your faculties focused on sensing their mood and reactions and on helping them to feel welcome, at ease, and at home.

Your role as host or hostess, however, must be assumed with moderation and tact. If overdone, potential friends will feel that they are being singled out for "special treatment," and will be chilled, not warmed, by your warmth. You must learn to live with the paradox, in a constant tension between the ideal and the practical reality.

The ideal, as stated by a Negro teacher, is "simply treat Negroes as people, indeed as any other human being." In practice, however, if you do this, you will not often get the same type of response you are used to getting with whites. Most colored Americans have had experiences of a type that probably few of your white friends have known, and you can usually expect to meet the results of these experiences somewhere along the line. Chapter 7 gives an extreme example of this paradox in action.

THE SEGREGATED SITUATION

If there are Negroes in your area but none in your neighborhood, school, or where you work, you may have to go out, as I did, and forage for congenial acquaintances across the color line.

In the Appendix there is a list of national organizations dedicated to civil rights and nondiscrimination. Some of them may be in your telephone book. If not, by writing to their headquarters you can learn which have chapters near you. Their membership is, of course, integrated and is made up of people who, like yourself, want to broaden their contacts in human relations. Joining one or more of them is a good way to start.

In tightly segregated areas with no integrated organizations near, it is well to begin by telephoning Negro ministers and school principals. You may find one who personally will help you make contacts. In any case, they can give you information about individuals and organizations in the Negro community who might help you.

What excuse can you give for calling them? Frankly tell them both your final aim and what you hope to get from them personally.

Will they not think you very strange? Yes, but probably very interesting. You will be doing what they think many white people should do. True, having learned to suspect the motives of whites, they will doubt your sincerity. (This is one reason why absolute frankness is essential.) But they will also want to believe you, and probably will give you a chance. Do not muff that chance—you may not get another.

How you phrase your request is important. Try not to let any of your segregated attitudes creep in. If you are a Southerner, be particularly careful not to sound paternalistic. Emphasis should fall on *your* need of help, not on your wish to help them in their fight for equality. Few Negroes any longer feel the need of white help. Many resent our assumption that they do.

Modern colored Americans often look upon us with pity— perhaps because it helps them not to hate us. They think of us as imprisoned within our own prejudices. Make use of that image if it fits your case.

Admit that you feel cooped up within your own group, cut off from the stream of humanity. Admit that you need help in getting free and in acquiring cosmopolitan relationships. Say you wish both to talk and work with people sympathetic to your aims. This language of a larger human life is better understood by most Negroes than by most whites.

If your appeal is made to a clergyman, ask whether you may attend his church; if made to a school principal, ask whether you may come to the exhibits and programs open to the public. But emphasize that you also want to meet congenial individuals who will help you break out of your white prison.

THE INTEGRATED SITUATION

If you live in a community, North or South, where some integration exists, your procedure will be different. Integrated organizations and predominantly Negro churches and schools may still be your best avenues of approach. In such cases it is better simply to appear at these places without comment. Your presence will create no sensation. Just act as though you belong, concentrate on being agreeable and useful, and you probably will be accepted—if you do not blunder too often.

Let us suppose that your school or job is integrated. That is an almost ideal setting for the establishment of intergroup friendships. You have built-in interests and conversation pieces, and there are no "racial implications" inherent in the situation, as there are when you appear at a place where you would not be ordinarily.

If you are already established at the school or job when colored students or workers begin there, it is even better. Then you can frankly seek them out and introduce yourself, as one merely courteously welcoming a stranger.

On the other hand, if they are established and you are the newcomer, you can still gracefully approach them as one needing information and advice. But be sure your manner is humble, even apologetic for bothering them, else they may suspect that you feel a Negro is naturally there to serve your needs. Let them see that you recognize their superior position as people who know the ropes; be grateful for crumbs they drop from their table of wisdom.

If you are in the position neither of serving a stranger nor of being one, and have no mutual acquaintance who might bring you together, your task is more difficult. Boldly to introduce yourself without excuse might create suspicions of the hated "special treatment." It is safer to move more slowly toward acquaintance.

Begin with a mere nod or smile in passing. A few days later include a brief "hello!" Then, a casual ejaculation, "What a day!" or "At last the weekend!" After this, if you introduce yourself at the first opportunity, it will seem more natural—and meaningful, too.

EARLY CONVERSATION

When at last you have a chance to talk, is it all right to say anything you would to any other stranger? On most topics, definitely yes. Probably, as with any stranger, the best thing to talk about is what you both are doing. If you are students, talk about your school. Tell about your classes, ask about theirs. Discuss the athletic and cultural programs. Try in your rambling to pin down their special interests and hobbies. Once you do that, you are off to a good start. Whether you can go on into real friendship from there depends on how much you have in common.

Will it really be that easy? It certainly should be; but when you come right down to cases, it may not. It will be easy precisely to the degree that you both are able to leap over your special preconditioning and stereotypes and to reach the awareness that in human relationships race has no existence and no place. The world of race and the world of human fellowship are different and irreconcilable worlds.

Successful friendship between white and colored Americans is like successful singing. Though perfectly natural, it still must be learned. It takes much vocal training to remove tensions that constrict voices. I hope the following pages will lift tensions from some minds and hearts.

4

INCLUSION IS
THE KEYNOTE

Following a try-out for a dance program at a Northern college, Hester Jean, a slender, dark skinned girl, was poised gracefully near the wings of the stage. Up bustled Sue, a beaming little redhead. Bubbling with good will in general and admiration for Hester in particular, she cried:

"I knew you'd have marvelous rhythm!"

"*How* did you know?" Hester asked.

"Why, colored people always have better rhythm than we do."

"Do you know I can sing, too?"

"I didn't. But colored people do have lovely voices."

Turning on her heel, Hester left without a word.

Sue looked stricken. "What did I say wrong? I meant to be nice!"

"I know, Sue," I said. "You were complimenting her. But for reasons I'm afraid we all must learn, something disagreeable you implied came through with more impact than your compliment."

RACE CONSCIOUSNESS

Sue's remarks revealed keen consciousness of race. They plainly said that Hester, being Negro, could be expected to have "racial characteristics." Even if aware of this, few whites would comprehend its offensiveness. Sue did not.

"Why," she demanded, "do they mind having their race remembered? We don't."

The answer lies in the experiences described in Chapter 1. Of course, we fail to share their yearning that race be ignored only because we have not been rejected, insulted, and denied fulfillment on the ground that we are white—though with the world fast shrinking and three-fourths of it nonwhite, we may have this experience before long. While some Negroes individually have escaped suffering from discrimination, all have a poignant awareness that it is the common lot of their people.

GENERALIZATIONS

Sue's remarks derived an additional sting from the fact that they were based on an ethnic generalization. When I pointed this out, again she was puzzled:

"They shouldn't be so touchy. People of other races *like* sweeping compliments about their race. We do. Chinese love to be told their race is wonderful. So do Jews."

"I'm glad you mentioned Jews," I said, "because they help my point. Although not a race but a religious group, many Jews do resent group generalizations, even when meant to be complimentary. And it's for the same reason that Negroes do: they, too, have been persecuted as a group for being 'different.' Though this has happened to segments of Chinese here and there, it hasn't happened to them as a whole people—or to us."

Generalizations have so often been used detrimentally—

Negroes are boisterous, childish, lazy; Jews, pushy, grasping, crude, and so forth—that the untruthfulness of all generalizations about people has been brought sharply to their attention. Moreover, they well know that historically and currently group generalizations and group exclusion are linked together.

Furthermore, since few Negroes have been allowed to achieve self-fulfillment regardless of ability, the group as a whole is forced to a lower cultural level than the white group. Thus a generalization implying that all are alike robs a gifted individual of respect earned under the most difficult conditions. Saddled with "racial traits," good and bad, he remains "just a Negro."

Then, too, generalizations are reminiscent of the costly and maddening claim of Southern whites: "We know the Negro." Blanket assertions about a group imply smug assumptions that we know what we are talking about. We can know nothing of the sort. No such creature as "the Negro" or "the white man" actually exists.

STEREOTYPES

Generalizations rest on fixed images, stereotypes. When we think in terms of group characteristics, we are, of course, seeing stereotyped images, not real people. We readily form these stereotypes when we are only in external contact with a group but have no actual friends among them.

Once formed, these images stand between us and the people we project them on, so that we can look straight at a real person and see only our stereotyped image instead. And he gets the miserable feeling of being blotted out as a person by our preconception.

It is hard to rid ourselves of stereotypes because we unconsciously collect evidence that supports them and reject that which does not. Always those things are most meaningful to us which tie in with familiar ideas. It is from this fact that the stereotype derives its power.

For instance, seeing Hester's performance, Sue thought, "Ah, how typical!" The fact was that only the day before a Negro student without a sense of rhythm had tried for the part and failed, but Sue made no mental note of that at all. It did not "fit the picture," was untypical, and therefore being unmeaningful, it was ignored.

At least Sue, being good willed, stressed "racial virtues" in her stereotype. The habit of seeing images instead of people is at its cruel worst when faults are crystallized in a stereotype. Then we get the "bad Negro"—or Jew or Catholic—image, from which lynchings and other persecutions result.

But even good stereotypes separate us from those on whom we project them. We cannot reach, touch, or know the real person, nor he us. It is for this reason that many Negroes resent the good stereotype as much as the bad.

WE AND THEY

It happened that Sue's very choice of words gave Hester a feeling of being set apart. To Sue colored people obviously were "they" who have this or that, in contrast to what "we" have. Most whites need deliberately to train themselves against this habit of pairing off words: we-they, we-you, ours-yours, ourselves-themselves.

To persons deeply aware of rejection by other groups, it is distressing to hear these proofs of inner segregation. Partly because they are used unconsciously, these paired-off words tell a sad story of walls standing in the hearts even of people who are seeking the destruction of those walls.

We must practice including colored citizens in our personal pronouns. They are not "those people" or "the Negroes." They are "*we* Americans." Civil rights is not, of course, "their chief problem." It is "*our* major American problem." And if we are Christians, it is "*our* primary concern that *we* heal the torn Body of Christ."

EXCLUSION AND INCLUSION

In seeking companions who are colored, the over-all point to keep in mind is that no one likes to feel excluded. A flattering reason for exclusion hardly helps. A student rejected by fellow students for being "too intellectual" often is almost as hurt as if he had been branded subnormal. Young people excluded from fellowship because of superiority sometimes even react by striving to shed it. Therefore, when Sue spoke in a way to make Hester feel set apart, it mattered little that the form of the remark was a compliment.

For generations Negroes have been dealt with as though they were less than human simply because of the distinction of race. They would, indeed, be something other than human if by now they did not prefer that this whole way of thinking be eliminated from everyday use.

If we had to choose one rule for tactful exchanges across the color line, it should be this: *Never by word or act imply that you are thinking of race.* Most of the many points we need to keep in mind in winning friends who are Negro are related directly or indirectly to this.

The naturalness of the reaction cannot be overstressed. Anyone—Negro, Jew, physically handicapped person, or genius—who, because of an inescapable "difference" in himself, has been automatically and consistently excluded from hopes and experiences open to most other Americans will develop longings for the kind of acceptance that is oblivious to that difference. Acts or comments that call attention to it, or that make him aware that others are thinking of it, will bring him the chill of isolation.

5

EARLY DAYS OF
FRIENDSHIP

A painful truth should now be evident, one made inescapable by the fact that most Negroes assume that whites have all along been as aware as they themselves are of the burdens imposed on them by segregation. This truth is that the *normal* reaction of colored Americans toward white Americans is one of resentment.

We shall often meet Negroes with chips so lightly balanced on their shoulders that even a cordial handshake knocks them off. If we lucklessly meet several in a row, we will be tempted to conclude that "Negroes are soreheads."

Some Negroes miraculously rise above the hostility we have earned, and respond to friendly advances from us with spontaneous warmth. Awed admiration is due them as triumphant individuals. To expect something similar from average members of their group would be unrealistic and unkind.

Moreover, we must realize that none can be entirely without sensitivities resulting from blanket discrimination. If some do not let us see them wince, we should not conclude that no pain is felt. Indeed, we are indebted to the angry ones who make no secret of the points and frictions of segregation that have rubbed them raw. They will teach us what the bravely silent do not.

HORSEPLAY

It should not be necessary to issue the following warning, but observation indicates that it is. Young people especially, but jocular types of all ages, often think it a mark of true fellowship to quip about race to colored friends. They delight in kidding remarks which would be regarded as fighting insults if spoken seriously or by a stranger.

At a teenage conference Ed and his colored roommate Carl went out to get wood for a marshmallow roast. Returning with his logs a few steps ahead of Carl, Ed sang out on reaching the cabin door, "Hey, fellows, there's an Ethiopian in the woodpile!"

They all roared with good natured laughter, and Ed dropped an affectionate arm around Carl's shoulders. The young people obviously meant no harm, and Carl turned up the corners of his mouth to show he understood. But it was clear to at least one close observer that Carl thought the crack as unfunny as the rest thought it hilarious.

Well knowing that such "wit" ordinarily would fetch them a black eye or fractured jaw, well-meaning but tactless whites often take the sickly grin of their friend as the measure of his affection and esteem for them. They may be right as to that. They probably are quite wrong that he feels no pain.

Many Negroes have been taught since early childhood that certain names, phrases, implications, and accusations are endured only out of cowardice, or if the alternative to enduring means uttermost loss. Can they help feeling twisted inside when a friend blithely uses one of these expressions?

DON'T BRING UP "THE PROBLEM"

The very heart of the over-all misunderstanding between members of our two groups may be the fact that whites, on the one hand, know nothing of what it is like to be a segregated Negro, and Negroes, on the other, find our abysmal ignorance incredible. Early in a relationship these two great areas of difference often are translated in the Negro into irritation and indignation, and in the white into frustration and bewilderment.

Even when he knows enough to eliminate all racial implications from his first conversations with Negroes, a Caucasian newly awakened to the problem of discrimination can hardly restrain his eagerness for the day when he can introduce the topic without giving offense. He yearns to hear at firsthand what it is like on the other side of the segregation wall, and he burns to express to his new friends his flaming views concerning it.

The subject, being fresh and exciting to him, is always in his mind, especially if he has corralled a victim of segregation. Insights concerning the problem rise in him like little geysers. It is cruel to tell him that he should not discuss it with a Negro friend. But with the exceptions soon to be noted, he certainly should not.

One reason is that a stereotype of the white man commonly held by Negroes pictures him as forever striving to embarrass, hurt, or put Negroes "in their place." For instance, I have before me a letter from a Negro friend who has just read a rough draft of this chapter:

"I am amazed at many of your statements of naivete," she writes. "Whites are deliberate in their mistreatment of Negroes. I firmly believe that most whites take sadistic pleasure in insulting Negroes. The chance bolsters their ego, makes them feel 'great'!"

Now this lady is an English teacher and a careful writer. When she says "most," she means *most*. If she had meant "some whites," she would have used the word *some*. Of course, her statement is as far from the truth as it would be to say, "Most Negroes would rape any white woman they could get to." Both statements are true only of a very small percentage.

However, "dragging in the problem" is often considered one of the deliberate sadistic acts that bolster white egos. Most Negroes much appreciate those rare whites who can spend hours in their company without referring to "the problem" in any way.

Few of us know that well-to-do Negroes, living in areas where segregation is illegal, sometimes feature never mentioning discrimination even among themselves. If you chance to talk with one of them, your introducing the topic may be taken as a flat insult—and may fetch you one in return. But even among those Negroes who continually discuss it with each other, a white person's reference to it will many times be greeted with wrath.

BEING NATURAL

It can be argued that one sure way to call attention to something is to make a great show of ignoring it. This can indeed be as bad as dragging it in—*if the other person is aware that you are avoiding it.* It is precisely here that the great gap between the newly integrated Caucasian and the average Negro comes into focus.

Everyone would agree that when the problem of discrimination thrusts itself naturally into the conversation, it should not be avoided. The split in opinion occurs on the matter of what is natural.

It is sadly natural for a newly integrated white to speak of it at times when most Negroes would think it unnatural. For the white, fellowship across the color line is such an exciting adventure that he cannot forget for one instant—nor does the novice want to—that he is talking to a Negro. Though perfectly normal in the tyro integrationist, this attitude is so shocking to many Negroes that it is a minimum courtesy not to confront them with it.

On the other hand, when the subject clearly obtrudes itself from without, it is awkward and wrong to ignore it. Suppose the newspaper you and your colored companion are looking at features the headline: RACE RIOT IN ————. He will expect you to give him a clue as to your feelings.

Do not imagine that your position will always be clear merely from your past behavior toward him. Many colored Americans have been taught that one can never determine a white man's thinking on this subject by his attitude toward individuals—a conclusion which events in the South and elsewhere have repeatedly demonstrated is sound.

Now is the time to state your views flatly, "Why are so many whites too dumb to see that when people are refused an equal chance, *of course* they'll eventually rebel?"

But although most Negroes want white acquaintances to keep off the subject of discrimination, I do not mean to imply that all Negroes feel the same about this—or anything else. Your particular friend may even try to lead you into declaring your position. If so and you do not respond, he will suspect the worst.

It is well to keep your ear to the ground for clues as to what he expects of you. As a general rule, if a Negro American makes any reference, no matter how oblique, to civil rights, prejudice, or discrimination in talking to a white stranger or casual acquaintance, he is feeling that person out and a statement of views is indicated.

You will be wise to form the habit of watching for chances to make clear your attitudes without ever introducing the topic of race. Frequent openings are provided by the daily news. Praise liberal figures for their courage; express approval when civil rights legislation is passed; refer to fine Negro leaders as great, brilliant, or effective; applaud the spirit shown by Negro demonstrators; release a blast at the latest segregationist in the news. All this can be done with no reference to race or "the problem," but only to the merit or lack of merit in the person or event in the news. Your friend will know what you mean, and if he wishes to introduce the topic himself, he will know he can.

EAGERNESS VERSUS BOREDOM

If the subject is prominent in the news or if your friend himself brings it up, you may think that it is all right to hash it over to your full satisfaction. After all, why not? None of the objections discussed above would apply now. True, but there are other traps.

This is a topic on which he probably is almost an expert, while you know next to nothing. All whites who have not been extensively instructed (and some who have) are stuffed with stereotyped images, misconceptions, and misinformation.

You can hardly open your mouth without saying something untrue, perhaps shocking to him. Remember that through personal involvement he is supersensitized to this whole body of errors. Your innocent but idiotic mistakes will fall on his raw nerves like a dentist's drill. At very best you will appear to him as being at your very worst.

This will be so even if you have read enough to avoid the worst falsification of facts. Your eagerness to talk about the subject is proof enough of its zestful newness to you, whereas your friend has been grinding it over all his life. Insights which are sparklingly fresh to you are dead and decomposed clichés to him. It would hardly be possible for you to say anything on this subject that the average Negro will not have heard *ad nauseam*.

GET ON HIS WAVE LENGTH

There is, however, one hope for you. *He may want to talk to you about it.* He may receive a kind of release in expressing himself to a white person. If so, you need not conceal the fascination you feel. You can ask all the questions you want. Try to draw him out. Encourage him to pour into your ear every thought and emotion which comes. If he wants to talk about it, it is because he needs to. Let him do the talking, and each of you can help the other to be free.

Let him see that you are sympathetic, concerned, yet keep your emotions carefully in balance. Take your cues from his own attitude toward what he tells you, and keep in step. Avoid taking the problem harder than he does himself. To do that can in itself be a separation between you—a kind of segregation. Worse, it can even border on pity. He wants you in there with him, identifying yourself with all that he feels, not way out front with your distress and concern.

6

WATCH YOUR
LANGUAGE

Chapter 2, you recall, reviewed certain words and phrases which through accumulated, painful association have become sore spots with America's largest minority. There are so many of these sore spots that sometimes, for the uninformed, effective communication is almost impossible. Your every remark seems to annoy! Yet, did you but know it, the remedy is ready to hand: precisely the same thought differently expressed may be highly acceptable.

Often the offense taken is justified, the word, phrase, or statement having been used in such a way as to reveal unconscious condescension or rejection on the white person's part. But it cannot be denied that now and again colored listeners read into perfectly acceptable remarks implications that really are not there. In either case, we must try to eliminate language that may be misunderstood.

JOKES

Let us hope that anyone reading this book would not be guilty of telling a joke, no matter how funny, with an American minority as its target. But many who would never do that know no better than to tell jokes which, although at the white man's expense, employ Negro dialect to make their point.

A classic example is the story about a certain Southern governor who is noted chiefly (I might say *only*) for segregationist efforts. It tells of his knocking confidently on the pearly gates, only to hear a voice from within inquire sweetly, "Who dat out dar?"

White integrationists often double up with laughter on first hearing this story. They see it as making, with delightful adroitness, the points that Negroes are spiritually on the inside and the governor is on the outside, his behavior toward them having ensured his being rejected when he arrives at heaven's gate. The dialect seems only a succinct way of identifying the gatekeeper as one unlikely to be inclined favorably toward the governor.

But few, if any, colored persons find the story funny. What seems to come through for them is the fact that it is by *mispronunciation* that the character is identified as Negro. I heard a white politician tell this joke to an all-colored audience, and I saw no smile break on any face. He garnered no votes from that speech.

It may be worth noting that one of the earliest symptoms of separation between minds is a separated sense of humor. Even when two individuals appear to understand each other perfectly in serious discussions of a topic, if they do not laugh at the same jokes about it, you may be sure that they are not seeing it in the same way.

White Southerners will be quick to point out that this constitutes proof that they and "their Nigras" see all things eye-to-eye, for they constantly laugh together. This would indeed be proof of understanding were it not for the fact that the welfare of the Southern Negro depends on his playing up to the white. He therefore often laughs at jokes which privately make him burn, and also cracks jokes he knows will please, even though he himself is not amused.

A white sometimes experiences a painful shock when he overhears Negroes who are unaware of his presence joking among themselves. It was quite a while after I imagined myself integrated before I was sincerely amused by most jokes I heard Negroes tell each other, especially if they were directed toward the South or Negro-white relationships.

PHRASES

In the next chapter it will be seen that phrases such as "good Negro" and "old Mammy" have an entirely different emotional content for whites than for colored Americans. A phrase that is innocently used by many white speakers yet consistently gives offense is "you people." Again and again I have seen colored audiences freeze when a totally friendly white speaker said, for instance, "As you people well know . . ."

With no exceptions that I know of, Negroes think the phrase stems from the state of mind discussed under the heading "We and They" in Chapter 4. In short, they take it for *mental segregation*, apparently through unawareness that it is commonly used by white speakers addressing white, as well as colored, audiences.

A few speakers may indeed use it patronizingly to mean "you Negroes," but in general it simply means "you persons whom I address," "you of the audience out there," and many grave injustices to liberal speakers have resulted from a failure to recognize this fact.

Yet the error is natural. Relatively few Negroes hear white speakers address white audiences, and when a white person uses the phrase in conversation with an individual Negro, he does, of course, mean precisely the duality—"we people," "you people"— from which colored American citizens justifiably shrink.

Another phrase guaranteed to antagonize any Negro concerned with civil rights—that is, if the topic is some aspect of the rights struggle and the phrase is employed as advice—is "slow down," or "go slow." This is likely to annoy even if your listener secretly agrees that extreme caution is needed lest gains already made be lost.

"Slow down" has been repeated with such a rhythmic beat by those determined to impede any progress toward equality that the phrase does not mean for colored what it often means for white moderates and integrationists, "Proceed with care." It means, "Delay indefinitely," "Suspend effort." Indeed, the very words *caution* and *care* when used by whites in this connection are quite loaded for Negroes.

If circumstances compelled me to try to convey this warning, I would attempt some such phrasing as "Let's quickly make new plans so that we will not be slowed down by the growing opposition." This would be about the only way that the warning not to blunder forward might possibly be issued successfully by a white.

"Might possibly," I say, for this is a case where not the phrases alone but also the idea behind them—even the whole area of thought—is emotion laden. Caution warnings from whites can hardly find acceptable expression. The present day Negro American does not intend that his momentum toward freedom be broken either by trick or timidity on the part of those who have been crying out, "Wait! Wait!" for more than a hundred years.

Set against the background of the delays and frustrations which he has repeatedly undergone, his determination not to halt for friend or foe is certainly understandable and usually sound as well. But even if it were not, there would be no arguing with it. It is as much a part of the aroused modern Negro as his vital organs. We must accept it along with him or reject him along with it.

SONGS AND LITERATURE

We who wish to wipe out barriers between white and colored citizens must also resign ourselves to banishing certain favorite songs and stories. If you are a Stephen Foster lover, for instance, you may croon "Jeanie with the Light Brown Hair" and "S'wanee River," but you may not even hum "Carry Me Back to Ol' Virginie" or "Ol' Black Joe."

Worse still, some Negroes repudiate spirituals—on the ground that they perpetuate stereotypes and associate Negroes with bad grammar. Others, who themselves thoroughly enjoy singing and hearing spirituals, recoil from them when they are introduced by whites.

At a recent important religious conference, integrated but dominated by whites, several Negro delegates almost walked out upon learning that a famous singer of spirituals had been chosen as entertainer. Yet some who were most indignant own all the albums of her records.

Their reaction probably stemmed chiefly from the Negro stereotype of the paternalistic white who, unfortunately, is much in evidence at such conferences. According to this stereotype the chief enjoyment such whites get from spirituals is amusement at what they consider "childishly emotional expressions in typical dialect"—*typical,* of course, being another loaded word. This stereotype depicts a person who feels for Negroes about 50 per cent rejection and 50 per cent sentimental condescension.

Condescension may well be what educated colored Americans detest and fear most from whites—detest, because it insults; fear, because it undermines their very will to achieve. Keeping this in mind may help us to accept, as just penance for the sins of our race, certain heartaches we shall receive.

Along with the trash of minstrel shows and romanticized stories of the antebellum South, great folk masterpieces of devotion, music, and literature must be thrown out, and among these —to some of us most loved of all—*Uncle Remus.* To us they may seem innocently beautiful; to many Negroes they recall a smarting, bitter past. In the midst of their fight for simple acceptance as human beings like other Americans, it is too much to ask that they retain anything which sets them apart. Later, when the fight is won, when all the walls we have built are leveled, then perhaps with pride and comfort they will reclaim some of the good grain they tossed out with the chaff.

NOTHING IS UNANIMOUS

All this is not to say that some Negroes even now do not stand against the tide of popular minority opinion regarding what to reject. Some—even many—do. Others stoutly maintain that the tide already has turned toward reclaiming rejected folk treasures.

Just here let me stress again the fact that popular minority opinion resists belief that *any*one speaks for the group. This stand is taken in opposition to the segregated white's assumption that all Negroes think alike. It is not well to ask, "What do Negroes feel" about thus-and-so? It is better gingerly to inquire, "Do you think many Negroes feel" thus-and-so? or "How do you think minority opinion is apportioned on this issue?" Still better, simply ask, "How do you think most people feel about this?" Your listener will understand that you mean the people he knows best.

So strong is the sentiment against generalizing about Negroes that one should unfailingly qualify statements about them with *many*, *most*, or *some*. T. J. Sellers, who was my teacher when I first turned down the road to brotherhood, put it this way:

"Negroes hate generalizations about themselves so much that you can't even say 'Negroes hate generalizations.' You have to say, '*Most* Negroes hate generalizations.'"

7

TYPICAL IMAGES

Jim and Eva Wilks went to more trouble to prepare for Dr. Karr's visit than they usually did for guests in their average Midwestern home. They wanted him to know that nothing was too good for him, that it was an honor to have him stay with them. Jim bought fresh roses for the dinner table and guest room, and Eva slaved all day getting the room ready, shining silver, making the house immaculate.

She rejected the temptation to prepare an easy dinner, choosing instead a menu of dishes most praised by former guests: fried chicken with cream gravy, mashed potatoes whipped with real butter and cream, tiny fresh peas cooked with mushrooms, homemade rolls, tossed salad and—to have one item which required little preparation—watermelon. By six o'clock she was exhausted but groomed to appear radiant.

At first the evening went just as the Wilks had hoped. When they showed Dr. Karr his room, he obviously was aware of and pleased by the numerous touches added for his enjoyment and comfort. As they sat chatting with cool drinks before dinner, gratitude spoke in his face and voice when he said:

"You can't imagine what it means, on this exhausting lecture tour, to have a taste of real home life and fellowship. Not many people are as kind as you to a near-stranger. In three weeks of constant travel, this is the first time I have stayed in a *home*." (He almost said a *"white* home.")

Talking later, Jim and Eva decided that the change in atmosphere began when they were discussing "the good old days" versus modern mechanization.

"All these labor saving devices don't take the place of another pair of hands," Eva complained. "My mother kept a better house than I and had more time, too—all because she had a houseboy and cook instead of a vacuum cleaner and an electric sink."

"Where did you live?" Dr. Karr asked.

"In Virginia. Help was cheap then, of course. What I paid for my vacuum cleaner and sink would have hired the best cook and houseboy in the county for more than a year. Dreadful— isn't it?—that people were expected to live on such wages!"

"The worst thing about mechanization," Jim put in, "is the loss of the human element. The . . . er . . . help"—he avoided the word *servants*—"in our household were loved as much as— maybe more than—most members of our family. My old . . . er . . . nurse"—he skirted the word *Mammy*—"was like a second mother to me."

"Where did *you* live?" Dr. Karr inquired.

"South Carolina until I finished high school. Then I went to Harvard. When I graduated I came straight here. Where did you go to school, Dr. Karr?"

"Harvard."

The conversation then moved on to the good old days at Harvard. But the early rapport, the warmth of fellowship, seemed gone. There was faint but growing tension in the air.

At dinner when Jim inquired which part of the chicken he would have, Dr. Karr's voice was a little chilly—or did Jim just imagine it?—when he replied: "No chicken, please. I'll stick with just vegetables." But he smiled into Eva's stricken eyes, and added politely, "These are my favorite vegetables."

Talk moved on without zest but smoothly until Eva brought on the dessert. "None for me!" he said quickly, and this time did not smile.

"You don't like watermelon? I'm sorry."

"I have a headache."

"Then you wouldn't care for some cake instead? I have angel food. Or maybe some canned fruit?"

"Either would be fine, thank you."

From then on conversation was so labored that Eva was glad when Jim suggested playing their new record. She leaned back, relaxed at last, as the rich voice of Marian Anderson floated out: "Swing low, sweet chariot, comin' for to carry . . ."

Dr. Karr rose. "My headache is worse, Mrs. Wilks. May I retire?"

"Oh, I'm so sorry!" Eva was on her feet, all concern. "Would you like some aspirin?"

"Thank you, no. I just need to be quiet."

REAL AND IMAGINED

This incident shows how a stereotype can destroy a budding friendship, but it has a surprise twist. It was Dr. Karr's stereotype of the Southern white, rather than Jim's and Eva's stereotype of the Negro, which ruined the evening for them all.

Neither Jim nor Eva did or said anything actually wrong. Trouble began when Dr. Karr, on discovering where his new friends were from, at once suspected them of typical Southern misconceptions. Seen through the glasses of his suspicion, their offenses multiplied until their company was insufferable.

The Wilks were kindly people who meant well, he conceded, but who could stand the dear-ol'-Mammy, faithful-servant image so cherished by paternalistic Southerners? The worst of it was that although he obviously did not fit this picture, they had projected it onto himself! It was evident that they saw him as a fried-chicken-loving (thus, maybe, even chicken-stealing!), watermelon-eating, spiritual-singing "ol' darky." And, by heaven! he told no lie when he said he had a headache—yes, and a sick stomach, too!

Although Dr. Karr may have been a little more suspicious than most Negroes of comparable culture, he was, of course, right in judging that a Virginian and South Carolinian might have such a stereotype of the Negro. He was even right in believing that the Wilks's's inviting him to stay with them did not *necessarily* prove that they had revised this stereotype, for Southern whites often reject segregation on moral grounds without changing their image of the Negro.

Therefore, although the chief error was indeed on Dr. Karr's part, Eva and Jim were much at fault for providing a setting in which such an error could easily occur. Moreover, had they been intelligently watchful, they could have nipped it in the bud, as we shall see.

THE MAMMY IMAGE

Nothing so annoys modern, educated Negroes as to have someone's dear old colored nurse held up as the epitome of Negro superiority. And many Southern whites regularly do it unless they have laboriously learned better.

In Southern imagery, dear-ol'-Mammy is a sort of feminine Uncle Tom, cabin and all. She is the "good Negro," whose superiority lies entirely in personality and character and whose chief traits are loving, faithful service and loyalty to her "white folks." This image allows neither for intellectual attainments nor for desire or ability to gain them.

That it contributed much to keeping the Negro "in his place" is certain. For with its aid whites of good will could remain unaware of the Negro's plight—could think of him as happy in service and so charmingly picturesque, loving and lovable that he should not be "spoiled" by acquiring sophistication, i.e., education. Loving their ol' Mammy, they wanted all Negroes to be like her—and imagined that all good ones were.

THE STEREOTYPE OF THE STEREOTYPE

Once having learned that the Wilks were Southerners and that Jim loved his ol' nurse, Dr. Karr saw, from then on, his own stereotype of the paternalistic white instead of seeing Jim and Eva. Had they been from Maine and Vermont instead of Virginia and South Carolina, he would have found nothing wrong with their behavior and would have continued to enjoy them as friendly individuals. Old nurses and family retainers are everywhere loved, regardless of color or national origin. This in itself certainly is no sin, provided one does not generalize on this basis and form a stereotype of the group to which the nurse or retainer may belong.

Jim and Eva did not do this. They were well aware that Negroes are capable of as high intellectual and cultural achievement as anyone. They had long ago learned to think of all people as individuals, and had laid aside false assumptions and poor attitudes in regard to all groups. Dr. Karr, however, did not see them as individuals but as white Southerners.

The incident illustrates the paradox mentioned in Chapter 3. Forgetting his inevitable sensitivities resulting from his experiences as a Negro, the Wilks talked and behaved with Dr. Karr just as they did with Northern white friends. This works only in theory. It was precisely because they failed to keep his background in mind that he was sure they were giving him "special treatment."

NOT WORDS ALONE

Needed on Jim's part was awareness of what Negroes have suffered from the Mammy image. His Northern white friends had kidded him about the word *Mammy* and he avoided it. But he did not know that the whole lovable-old-servant concept has become a "badge of rejection" to colored citizens. The mere statement, "They were more loved than any member of my family," is a cliché that makes most Negroes bristle. It reminds them of all the false assumptions which traditionally accompany this form of love in the South. Another cliché phrase which Jim used was, "My nurse was like a second mother."

Jim could have made his point about the importance of the human element without using phrases that have become badges of rejection: "In our household the work was not done by electricity but by real people whom we could know and love, and this enriched our lives." Expressed this way, Jim's thought probably would not have caused Dr. Karr's stereotype of the white Southerner to leap between him and his new friends.

STARVE THE IMAGE

Had Eva been more conscious of Dr. Karr's background, she might have chosen a steak-and-chocolate-éclair dinner instead of a chicken-watermelon one. But she still could have served her chicken dinner successfully if only she had casually mentioned that she was serving her "most complimented menu." Then Dr. Karr would have known that she had not selected those dishes especially for him on the assumption that they were appropriate for a Negro. As a matter of fact, like most people, he liked chicken—and watermelon, too.

The record Jim played was an LP collection of favorite old and sophisticated new songs sung by the best voices of today. Only two spirituals were included and only about 15 per cent of the singers were colored. If Jim had not quite forgotten that Dr. Karr was a Negro, he would have first played the other side, thus making a safe start with "Annie Laurie."

So we must all *live with the paradox of forgetting race, yet never forgetting that every colored American has had certain painful experiences because of his race.* We cannot hope to have successful relationships across the color line unless we learn to keep both these balls always in the air.

We must not only shed our own stereotypes of Negroes, but also we must learn what their stereotypes of white people are. And we must learn the various words, phrases, and habit patterns which Negroes take for evidence that we are thinking in stereotypes.

We must remain alert for the first sign that a stereotype is being thrust between ourselves and a friend. It may be ours or his. No matter. In either case, by breaking up the overfamiliar patterns of words and thoughts, by avoiding doing and saying what is expected next in terms of the stereotype, and by doing or saying the unexpected instead, we can starve the stereotype to death. For it is the unchallenged old idea and habit, the unchallenged cliché, upon which it feeds.

8

INTEGRATION BAFFLEMENT

Like many white people who have left the South (and some who have remained), Jim and Eva Wilks had shed their special Southern misconceptions of Negroes and had come to think of them as just people. The trouble was that they had done so by reading and by discussions with enlightened Northern friends.

These friends did include a few Negroes, but they were Negroes whose families, because of financial and professional success, had suffered little oppression. Thus they were less sensitive and suspicious of whites than most colored Americans. If the Wilks pained them occasionally, the pain was not severe enough to require expression. So Jim and Eva were never informed when they made unwise or untactful remarks—until along came Dr. Karr. That was why they could not guess what ailed him or what to do about it.

This was their first experience of what I call "integration bafflement," a disease not fatal but distressing. Knowing that their hearts made no distinction between Negroes and whites, they were bewildered before Dr. Karr's increasingly obvious coldness and hostility.

FIND A TEACHER

In their place, I would have asked him flatly what was the matter. At that point there was nothing to lose, and he might have told me. If one has a bad case of integration bafflement, there is no cure, in my judgment, but overt forthrightness.

"I've tried and tried to get along with one Negro after another," Helen Dale told me one day. "I just can't. When I talk to them, they either bristle or freeze. I've decided simply to let them alone."

"Oh, don't do that!" I pleaded. "We need each other's friendship, and the nation needs us to be friends—the world does. Don't you see you're letting yourself develop prejudice where you were only ignorant before? You can't let that happen."

"How can I help it?"

"You can do what I did," I told her. "Find a teacher who'll show you what's wrong. Start with the Negro who seems to dislike you most. Ask him to explain why you make him burn."

This advice I often give. When it has been taken, I have not known it to fail. If most Negroes you approach seem cold or rude, you are probably much in need of instruction. Bluntly to ask for it may be your best move.

What of the rule, "Don't bring up the problem"? If you already offend whenever you speak, it is because you are unintentionally functioning as the problem itself: your very presence brings it up.

It is not, of course, invariably the white person's fault (though it usually is) when he offends. Resentment of whites is a neurosis with some Negroes, and when dealing with one of these, we must realize that he actually wants to be offended. We fight a lost battle in trying to please him.

But if, like Helen, we are at bay with many Negroes, then we can be sure that it is a case of "everybody's out of step but Johnny." We will do well to seek help.

WHAT WE WILL LEARN

What can we expect to learn from a Negro teacher? Broadly, two things: how we misunderstand Negroes, and how they misunderstand us. The process of learning both may be rather painful.

We should try not to challenge our teacher on his conclusions about us. Regardless of how untrue they may seem, we should suffer most accusations silently, for at least four reasons:

1. This task is difficult enough for him without our constantly disputing points he tries to make. He is our teacher, and like other teachers he should be respected. He knows something we do not know, or we would not have sought his aid.

2. If we listen patiently and thoughtfully, we may learn in what ways a Negro is likely to misunderstand us. This will be as valuable as learning what our own intergroup misunderstandings and misdemeanors are. If we question him respectfully about behavior on our part which he takes (perhaps unjustly) for symptoms of poor attitudes in us, we may learn how to avoid giving false impressions.

3. If he is often wrong and we convince him of it, we may lose him as a teacher. He will feel that his position is ridiculous.

4. Perhaps most important of all is the fact that on many points where, at first, we sharply disagree with him, we may agree later when we know more. When we are first accused of an unconscious bad habit, sharp denial is the normal reaction. We invariably think, "I certainly do *not!*" Later we may add, "Well, maybe *occasionally* I do." Finally, if we have learned our lesson, we murmur, "I'm afraid you're right."

So for both our teacher's and our own education's sake, we must not be problem pupils.

One of the things which should be kept in mind when talking with any Negro about "the problem" is that there is something humiliating about admitting that one has himself been humiliated. Therefore, it usually is well to make our inquiries concerning what happens to Negroes under segregation as impersonal as possible.

SEEKING A TEACHER

As we said earlier, in seeking a teacher, try to choose one who seems quite hostile toward you, perhaps the most hostile one you know. You want the truth, and he will be most likely to tell it to you. Without wasting time on working around to the subject, bluntly but humbly say:

"I fear in some ways my education was sadly lacking. My intentions are good but my behavior seems not to match them. I need help. Just now I meant to be pleasant. Please tell me *frankly* why I didn't succeed."

No need to be discouraged if you get nowhere on your first two or three attempts. Keep trying another person, then another. Not everyone can analyze his reactions, and the persons you first approach may not themselves know why you ruffle them. The sum of their feelings may merely be "I hate white people!" and they may not think it well to pass this along to you as a clue.

But most intelligent Negroes have thought much about intergroup relations. You probably will not search long before finding one who knows why you rub him the wrong way. He may be glad to inform you, may yearn to tell a white how to act. If so, there is real hope for you, and perhaps for him, in the telling.

The maze of segregation has become so much a part of the subconscious of most whites that our reactions and thought patterns automatically separate people into categories of black and white without our being aware of it. There is but one sure way to gain awareness: have a person who is very conscious of—because irritated by—what you say and do, make it his business *unfailingly* to rebuke you when you slip into these sins of separation.

When you find one willing to help you, be prepared for his painful frankness, even fraught at times with hostility. This may be the best way for you to learn. It is likely to be the only way he can teach. You will be a slow and trying pupil, having so much to unlearn before you can learn.

The task of laboriously instructing a white in what the teacher himself is sick of knowing is one which perhaps only an angry person will undertake. His payment as teacher will be largely the therapeutic release of bawling you out. But if for him you can be a symbol of all the whites who have misunderstood and tormented Negroes down the centuries, you both may profit greatly—he in therapy, you in learning—and the canyon of misinterpretation which divides white and colored Americans may be spanned.

9

THE HAUNTED HOUSE

"Why do most whites think we're eager to marry them?" This inquiry is a recurrent one in the Negro group.

"Isn't there danger that integration will increase intermarriage?" This question is asked continually in the white group, and the word *danger* often has a heavy ring.

WHY THE TERROR?

Fear of intermarriage is compounded of myth, tradition, indoctrination, misinformation, and neurosis. But that is not all. Realistic, practical considerations are included.

It may well be that the mingling of apparitional with real elements is responsible for the confusion and exaggerated fear that surround the subject. I doubt if anyone, white or colored, is altogether free of this confusion.

A person caught in a fear of intergroup marriage is like a superstitious man forced by a night storm into a house supposed to be haunted—but where a real gangster hides. As the lightning flashes and the tattered curtains and cobwebs wave, the man sees ghostly apparitions. He might force himself to accept these as imaginary, did he not also hear and glimpse a flesh-and-blood gangster creeping about. He might feel able to contend with the gangster, did his eerie hallucinations not turn his muscles to jelly. When the gangster craftily dons a horrifying Halloween mask, his victim's panic is complete.

In this chapter we shall deal with the apparitions and the mask. In Part Two we shall consider the real gangster.

THE APPARITIONS

Ask a tense-faced segregationist what he means by "the danger of miscegenation" and he is likely to retort, "The ultimate destruction of our country! Do you want us to become a brown nation?"

We could reply, "Why not? It would save time and money now spent on getting suntanned." But as our colored population is only 10 per cent and as most of its members already have noticeable amounts of Caucasian blood, even after complete amalgamation we probably still would have to resort to sunlamps and beaches for our attractive tans.

On learning this, our segregationist may cry, "When race mixing occurs, civilizations invariably fall!"

True. But of equal significance is the fact that people who move into brick houses invariably die—all within a few decades, some within a few months! Civilizations do fall, but reputable modern historians find no connection between "race mixing" and their demise.

"Biology shows," our segregationist will declare, "that cross-breeding produces offspring inferior to those of pure racial strains."

The best reply to this fiction is to ask for one biology text-book currently used by accredited colleges that makes such a claim relative to races of man. Anthropologists inform us sharply that "pure racial strains" exist only in the imagination. Race mixing began before the dawn of history.

MORE "DANGER" IN SEGREGATION

"Well," the segregationist may sigh, "if intermarriage must come, I hope I'm dead when it does."

Congratulate him—he probably will be. While experts who venture prophesy on the subject disagree, the consensus seems to be that integration will not speed amalgamation much or soon.

In towns with large Negro populations where segregation laws have never existed, few intergroup marriages occur. They often seem to be more numerous than they actually are because color contrast makes the couples conspicuous. Half a dozen in a city may appear, as they move about, to be scores.

How can there be much intermarriage when most people are physically attracted more to members of their own group, and when the widely divergent psychological conditioning in the two groups also creates a natural barrier? Except in rare cases, we all strongly tend to mate with those of similar backgrounds. Consequently, even those who fear intermarriage most have little reason to use it as an argument against integration.

Indeed, some experts think that segregation more than integration leads to intermarriage. Anthropologists have estimated that about 20 thousand Negroes who are light enough to pass for white "cross over" every year to escape the handicaps of segregation. They marry unsuspecting whites.

"The irony of it," a social psychologist commented, "is that Negroes who cross over often pretend to be rabid segregationists as a safeguard against detection. The result is that they attract genuine rabid segregationists as mates—people who would be utterly horrified if they knew."

One of the logical replies to the question "Do you want your daughter to marry a Negro?" might well be "Do you want your daughter to know a Negro suitor when she sees one?"

THE FRIGHT MASK

So much for the apparitions. Let us now consider another factor. Though neither hallucination nor practical obstacle, this factor so greatly heightens emotion and confuses thought that it prevents a calm appraisal of both imagined and real hazards of intergroup marriage.

Many, if not most, whites and a smaller percentage of Negroes are repelled by each other's "typical" physical characteristics. Here is one Negro's comment on Caucasian features:

"Whites have knife-edge lips, protruding noses which look squeezed in a vise, and flesh like that of a chestnut worm. The very thought of contact with them would give any normal man the creeps."

This man's scalp prickles and his blood boils if someone asks, "Would you want your daughter to marry a white?" For— let us face it—that question often inspires (and is prompted by) a very crude image in action. Thought of the sweet, softly rounded, golden-brown features and limbs of his little darling being ravished by the repulsive creature just described is enough to drive this loving father to visions of his shotgun.

Likewise, with reference to very dark, flat-nosed, protruding lipped Negroes, the epithet "black apes" seems to many whites less a random insult than an apt descriptive phrase. Harrassed by that image in action, the white father, too, envisions his shotgun. Worse, if he is criminally inclined and lives in the South, he may reach for it.

GUILT FEELINGS HEIGHTEN AVERSION

Physical aversion to certain features is a psychological fact. It is common to all and is not serious if we accept it as just that —the individual reaction of one person to the physical appearance of another. It is heightened and reinforced if we generalize from it and interpret it as racial, then go on to condemn it as prejudice or approve it as instinct. Actually, it is neither prejudice nor instinct but merely personal taste.

True, your personal taste is conditioned by what you are used to seeing within your own group. But that does not change the fact that the reaction itself is simply a direct esthetic response to physical actualities. It does not result from a stereotype, generalization, or misinterpretation. The person really has a flat nose and you dislike flat noses—*on anyone*. You probably dislike them more on whites than on Negroes.

And, no, you need not fear that you dislike them only because you associate them with another race. When a white man has a flat nose and protruding mouth, other whites seldom say, "He looks like a Negro," but rather, "He looks like an ape."

QUALIFYING IS ALL RIGHT

It makes no difference how liberal or free from prejudice you are, if you are confronted with the question "Would you want your daughter to marry a Negro?" you cannot answer honestly with a simple *yes*. Your reply must be qualified because circumstances are all important.

Yet most white liberals feel painfully guilty if they fail to produce a resounding, unqualified *yes*. Such a failure, both they and most Negroes feel, means that the individual still harbors prejudice and falls far short of the goals of brotherhood. This would be so if all reasons for hesitating rested on the hallucinations of racial bias. They do not.

In Part Two we shall examine this point in more detail. Here we need only stress that one qualification which we must be honest enough to admit necessary is that our son-in-law's appearance meet at least our minimum esthetic needs.

Naturally, a parent pulls back from thought of his child marrying a type that to him is physically repulsive—even if the person has a brilliant mind and noble heart. This simple, normal reaction should not be confused with prejudice. Many a white individual would also be repugnant as a son-in-law—for example, anyone who is very over or under weight.

NONCHALANCE TO THE RESCUE

I know a distinguished white author who looks like a cow, a tycoon who looks like a pug dog, a dedicated clergyman who looks like a bird of prey. My antipathy for their physical aspects is a fact, but it is also irrelevant in evaluating their essential human worth. That their appearance offends my esthetic sense is neither their fault nor mine; and if I sit in judgment neither on them nor myself, I can fully enjoy the charm and admire the skills displayed in many other aspects of their being.

My distaste becomes reprehensible only if I allow myself to imagine that these gifted people are cow-, dog-, or hawk-like in their total being. It becomes fiendish if I generalize and conclude that authors as a group are cowlike, and so forth.

Aversion for certain physical features often to be found in other races is best dealt with when it is accepted in this sensible relaxed way. It does not belong in the category of prejudice unless it is projected as the generalized image: "Negroes look like apes." That, of course, is ridiculous. Many jet-black Negroes no more resemble primates than does Miss America. To allow the ape image to encircle this nation's colored people (who are more varied in appearance than whites) is to approach the psychotic.

Anyone tormented by the ape image when thinking of inter-group marriage should practice projecting the Eartha Kitt or Harry Belafonte image, instead. And he may be sure that in the very unlikely event that his daughter should choose a mate across the color line, her choice would fall in the latter, not in the ape-image category.

When physical aversion obtrudes in an otherwise agreeable

relationship, do not think yourself unregenerate. If these quite innocent esthetic reactions are repressed, they may explode in intense repulsion. Guilt feelings denote more prejudice than does physical aversion. If a favorite relative, professor, or colleague reminds us of, say, a woodchuck, do we not feel less guilty than affectionately amused?

Physical endorsement is not necessary to healthy human relationships. That is what makes them human.

HOW TO JOIN THE HUMAN RACE

We have come to the end of Part One. While it was proper in this last chapter to say something about intermarriage, the most bewildering area of intergroup relations, let us, in closing, turn our minds once more to the broader horizon: how to function as total human beings—persons who seek each other, caring for one another.

There is a simple technique that helps us see people of any color, background, or persuasion simply as people, and basically just alike. It consists in habitually pretending that each person is of the opposite race from the one he really is. *When talking to, or thinking of, a Negro, pretend he is white; when dealing with a white, pretend he is Negro.*

Practiced daily, this habit reduces confusion, tension, doubts, and fear. It helps Negroes to believe in a friend who is white, and helps whites to forget that a friend is Negro, yet to recall that his heart has known a Negro's pain.

It mercilessly unveils our own stereotypes, then breaks their backs—making room for living people in our hearts.

PART TWO:

FOR COLORED ONLY

INTRODUCTION

In Part One we chiefly discussed the way certain white stereotypes and behavior patterns affect many Negroes. That is, I undertook to step inside the Negro's mind, identify with him, and bring other whites in with me.

Not being Negro, any success I had in that presumptuous effort could result only from wide experience and careful observation on the human relations front. Learning to see the world as members of another group see it requires much talking, working, and suffering with them.

But in Part Two, I am on home ground and can speak at firsthand. Here I discuss how stereotypes and behavior patterns found in many Negroes affect most whites. Obviously, I am better qualified for this task than the other.

Thus, anyone who thinks Part One deserves to be taken seriously by whites (especially if it makes them uncomfortable) must logically concede that Part Two should be taken seriously by Negroes (especially if it makes them uncomfortable). A mirror was held up in Part One for whites to see how they often make Negroes feel. The mirror now will be held up for Negroes to see how they often make whites feel.

Some of the points made in Part Two may be less familiar

to colored Americans than those made in Part One. For that reason, the points may seem less true. To some readers a few of the ideas may be quite new, and it is human nature to reject new ideas, particularly if they concern habitual unconscious errors of our own. Were all my Negro readers guilty of the mistakes described, it might seem futile to write Part Two. But I think many will be detached enough from the mistakes to recognize them.

Until the segregation wall began to crumble, there was little use in calling attention to these mistakes. When even Negroes who were singularly warmhearted and outgoing toward whites could not get over the wall, it made little difference that many Negroes had prejudices and attitudes that would make intergroup fellowship impossible.

But the picture has changed. We are coming together. Many non-Southerners will shortly meet Negroes for the first time. Many Southerners will meet Negroes as equals for the first time. On the nature of these meetings depends our future progress toward becoming a whole nation. If the experiences are pleasant, integration will move smoothly, gain momentum. If unpleasant, we will continue to creep at the pace of a lame snail.

1

POISONED WOUNDS

Suddenly Judy Daniel realized that the spring semester was almost over at a nearby college, and the two Negro students, of whom she was very fond, would soon graduate. She was working eighteen hours a day meeting deadlines on certain assignments, and besides that, her funds approached zero; so entertaining was not indicated. But she could not let her young friends leave town without having them to dinner once more.

So she wrenched her budget, drew on her reserve strength, and managed to fix a rather special meal for her family of four and two guests. Weary but full of warm anticipation, she arranged flowers and set up the TV trays on their individual tables in her small, quietly arrayed living room.

THE LETDOWN

Judy's delight at seeing her friends was quickly blighted. From the moment they entered the house something was wrong. A kind of angry gloom was thick in the atmosphere. Throughout dinner, host, hostess, and their two sons labored to keep conversation from withering entirely away.

Judy felt grieved for her family, and guilty. The guests were her friends, and the family should not have to suffer this dreary, tension-filled meal. She was glad that after dinner both husband and sons had previous engagements that took them away.

When they had gone, suffering in silence not being one of Judy's virtues, she asked the students to please tell her what was the matter. They answered honestly, and for that she was grateful.

"When we came in and saw those TV trays set up again," one said, "we almost turned around and walked out."

"Why?" She was bewildered.

THE EXPLANATION

With little further prompting, both poured out their thoughts. Clearly, they had long brooded and talked over their other dinner at Judy's house. It had, they admitted, been the first meal they had eaten in a white person's home, and the experience had fallen far short of what they had hoped.

Knowing how long and hard their hostess had worked on the human relations front, they had taken it for granted that she would make no distinctions between themselves and other people. They had been disappointed.

"How? In what way?" Judy asked, baffled. "What distinctions did I make?"

"Neither of us ever even heard of guests being treated the way you treated us. There's only one explanation: you don't want to sit at table with us."

TV trays! Individual tables! Now all was clear.

"Believe me," Judy said weakly, "I always use TV trays when I have guests. I'd use them even if the President and First Lady came to dinner. And I honestly don't think they'd mind."

The students exchanged incredulous glances. "We've compared notes, and neither of us has ever been out to dinner, even in the poorest home, where the table wasn't spread with a nice cloth. We always ate and talked together around a table—always.

And the best of everything the family had was always used."

As Judy listened to their carefully considered case against her, she felt as if her heart were being twisted and released, twisted and released.

MANY KINDS OF PAIN

Her distress at their misinterpretation was braided of many threads of pain. One was simply the disappointment of a hostess who, having spent time, strength, and bank account in an all-out effort to give her guests pleasure discovers she has failed.

Another was the deeper, more lasting ache of having reached out with her heart to others, thinking they shared her joy in the fellowship, only to learn that they viewed her with suspicion and wrath. Such an experience tears at the very roots of confidence in ourselves and joy in others. "What kind of impression do I really give?" we ask ourselves fearfully. And even more fearfully, "How can I know when others are my friends?"

Negroes are well aware of this experience in their own lives. They are less aware that it happens across the segregation wall, too.

Still another thread of pain was the embarrassment of one who has offered simple hospitality and learned it was judged not good enough. The students' reaction amounted to rejection of the way Judy lived. The house had no dining room. The breakfast nook seated only four. True, the living room possessed a drop-leaf table, but she had thought it easier and more pleasantly informal to use TV trays on the rare occasions when she had dinner guests. She had entertained this way for many years with no suspicion that anyone might criticize it. Now she wondered miserably how many people had.

Wounded vanity also struck its blow. She had taken pleasure in imagining it a bit of a thrill for two young people—as at their age it would have been for her—to be invited to the home of one who, though of modest means, was well known in her field. Letters and long distance calls often came to her from strangers in distant places asking to meet her, and usually she had to reply regretfully that she could not work it into an already overcrammed schedule. Now—when she had surrendered a much-needed afternoon and evening to prepare for and entertain these young people—she learned that they almost "turned round and walked out."

SYMBOL OF THE OVER-ALL PROBLEM

I review all this to show how many ordinary assumptions and hopes are blasted for white, as well as colored, Americans when race consciousness is injected by one or the other into a friendly relationship. In Judy's case, above and beyond these personal bruises, an enervating realization dragged from her the words:

"For more than a dozen years I've been dedicated to integration—and both of you know it. You've heard me speak on radio and television; you've read my writings on the subject, talked with me, visited here; yet *still* you don't trust me even as far as a TV tray! If even people like us can't understand each other, what hope is there for integration? I feel as though I've wasted all the years I've worked on it. I feel in absolute despair."

Later she recalled with tenderness their efforts to comfort her; yet the sum of all they said was that she could forget the whole thing now, for they were convinced of her innocence, they suspected her no more.

Forgiving them was no problem. She was fond of them, and so it was easy to disconnect them in her heart from what they had done. But their action had unveiled certain truths. Asking her to forget it was like asking a child to forget that he overheard his parents laughing at him, or a sweetheart to forget a lover's unfaithfulness. Something had been learned which changed the look of things.

Colored Americans seldom are aware that they, as well as whites, can deliver poisoned wounds that work chemical changes in the body which receives them. Young whites go to meet darker brothers full of joy and naive hope of rich new relationships to come. After a time they often totter back, tired and sad-eyed by defeat, to creep within the friendlier walls of their own group, and not to emerge soon, if ever again.

WE DEAL WITH PERSONS, NOT ABSTRACTIONS

Yes, the white man is responsible for the state of mind with which the Negro stabs him. But when an individual person is dealing with another individual, such a statement is meaningless and misleading. *"The white man" does not in fact exist, and neither does "the Negro." These are mere abstractions. Only persons exist.*

The British oppressed the American colonists; men have oppressed women; Christians have oppressed Jews; and white Americans have oppressed colored Americans. All groups with power and opportunity oppress other groups. This only underscores the eternal truth that man is sinful and shows that we all must work together for laws and customs that will compel and encourage a better society. The general human tendency to oppress has no bearing on the character, intentions, or potential for friendship of individual people.

Individual whites have inherited segregation just as Negroes have, and many are doing more to dissolve the barriers than probably any Negro you personally know. Great Negro leaders, of course, are doing more than any white. But the individual white who seeks your friendship is acting against current custom, thus proving his determination to make brotherhood a reality.

Such a determination, you may be sure, finds expression in

other ways that you do not see and is paid for in losses to him of which you will never know. On the other hand, how many Negroes do you personally know who have done more to usher in brotherhood than simply to talk resentfully about the lack of it? As with whites, only a minority of Negroes exert themselves for the welfare of all.

"The white man oppresses the Negro." Yes. But Tom Smith, Sally Jones, and Dr. Hall never have oppressed a Negro or anybody else. If one of them seeks friendship with Jim Carter, who is Negro, is it relevant in their case what "the white man" or "the Negro" has done?

2

WHY IT HAPPENED

What happened between Judy and these students spotlights the strong barriers to understanding which can divide good-willed white and colored Americans. These barriers are constructed out of stereotypes, misconceptions, and misinformation from *both* sides of the segregation wall.

THE STEREOTYPE OF PERPETUAL PREJUDICE

One stereotype of the white held by many Negroes pictures prejudice springing eternally in the chalky breast. Consequently, the integrated white often suffers more from the nagging suspicions of some of his colored friends than he does from the inevitable disapproval of unenlightened members of his own group.

If we examine the facts objectively, it should be clear that it is far easier for an emotionally stable white to change his racial attitudes than it is for a Negro to change his. A normal white's misconceptions of the other group are certain to be more on the mere intellectual level and less fraught with emotion than those of a normal Negro.

Whites have not suffered at dark hands as Negroes have at white hands, and thus no deep wells of repressed fury toward

Negroes normally exist. They have been told certain things about Negroes (which have not been supported by actual experiences), and they have absorbed by osmosis certain assumptions (which, again, have not been backed up by firsthand facts in most cases). All this, like other secondhand learning, can easily be corrected and revised through the *right kind of personal experience.*

Take my own case. Like most upper- and middle-class Southern white children of my generation, I was allowed to play freely with colored children. And as I was largely in the care of colored help, I saw more of Negroes than I did of whites. All— please note this—all my contacts with colored people were pleasant. Negroes were gentler, kinder, more courteous to me than white people were. Their economic and personal welfare was closely related to their popularity with white children, and they made the most of this agreeable form of social security. Even a person having only a casual knowledge of psychology knows that the inevitable result of such experience for these white children when they grow up will be a foundation of good feelings toward Negroes.

On top of this foundation of pleasant personal experiences the teachings of my region concerning race were laid like a veneer. I learned to think, talk, and behave as though Negroes were small, often naughty children. But my feelings toward them were good and remained good. Later I had only to learn how to give these feelings a proper setting and expression.

This is true of a vast number of Southern whites who only externally follow the variety of bad habit patterns that they were taught. Their interior little resembles their surface, and the belief that their prejudices are set in diamond-hard cement is as false as the white stereotype that Negroes are childlike.

Outside the South the situation is quite different. There, the Negro is not the familiar "child" but perhaps a total stranger, a "foreigner." No heartwarming memories of an integrated childhood exist, but whites who feel general good will toward men automatically include Negroes in it. Though they may have absorbed common stereotypes and unconscious assumptions of Caucasian superiority, they willingly—if they are emotionally healthy—discard these poor attitudes upon becoming aware of them.

In other words, anywhere in the nation the normal white who has had no painful personal experiences with Negroes can discard his racial veneer with comparative ease. Indeed, once Caucasians take the leap across the color line and become used to equality relationships with dark skinned people, they often achieve an unconsciousness of color which would gratify any Negro, could he believe in it. He seldom can.

HOSTILITY TOWARD NEGROES NOT NORMAL

Much hostility toward Negroes does, of course, exist and is often expressed; a few continually express it and in the most vicious ways. But with few exceptions, whites who are genuinely hostile toward all Negroes are emotionally disturbed persons who are also hostile toward most members of their own group.

This fact, though clear cut, is not obvious for reasons too numerous and involved to review here. But one or two need to be cited. The first is that laws and customs of an evil system make it horribly easy for persons who hate nearly everybody to vent that hatred solely on colored citizens.

Another is that much conduct on the part of whites which appears to Negroes to stem from hostility, results in fact (1) from pure ignorance of the effect on Negroes of such acts; (2) from fear of social reactions in other whites; and (3) from complete misunderstanding of the motives and intentions of a particular Negro, or group of Negroes, in a given situation.

THE STEREOTYPE OF WHITE LUXURY

The tap root of the students' misinterpretation of Judy probably was their stereotype of whites stuck forever in preju-

dice. But another factor may also have loomed large: the stereotype—common among Negroes—of white people living in a
more formal and luxurious way than they actually do. A great
deal of trouble stems from this frequent misconception. Occasionally, even, a snobbish Negro loses all respect for a white acquaintance upon visiting him, concluding that this person falls
far short of his group's standards and borders on "poor white
trash."

The origin of this stereotype is not hard to trace. Under
segregation Negroes gain access to white homes only as servants.
Persons who can afford household help naturally indulge in more
formality and luxury than the rest of us.

The majority of Negroes, even those now living elsewhere,
came originally from the South. A couple of generations ago,
wages being shamefully low, virtually all upper- and middle-class
Southern whites had full time household help. With a maid to
do the serving, formal service, even at family dinners, is a pleasant custom; and gleaming linen tablecloths and napkins are no
problem when a laundress is ready to hand.

In my childhood home, even on my father's modest clergyman's salary, all meals were served to us in the dining room on a
linen-covered table. But it took my mother only a brief time to
shift gears into kitchen eating, sans linen, when World War I
pushed wages up beyond the family means.

As luxury-living became increasingly difficult for Southern
whites, fewer and fewer Negroes saw the inside of their homes.
The homes they did see still had servants and other luxuries. So
the image of the white man living in style was passed on (no
doubt much exaggerated) to many children who, like Judy's
student friends, had never seen the inside of a white home.

NEGROES HAVE A HIGHER LIVING STANDARD

Wherever segregation, legal or *de facto*, prevents mingling,
there has been more of a tendency among Negroes toward formal

and luxurious living than there is among whites of comparable income. As their economic situation improved, many colored Americans perhaps tried to meet the standard they thought the white man still enjoyed. No doubt, they also were reacting to the white stereotype of Negro living standards being very low. Add to this the tendency of all people rising from extreme poverty to pull away from the conditions and habits of their past, and one could almost predict that well-to-do Negroes would strive to maintain higher standards of living than whites of equal income would.

However, the reasons for this divergence in custom concern us less here than the fact that many misunderstandings have resulted from it. When one group's stereotypes of the other create expectations that are not fulfilled when people from these groups come together, the result, as with Judy and her student friends, can be very painful for all involved.

A NATION WITHIN A NATION

Everywhere in the United States there are many customs, important and unimportant, that are common among and taken for granted in one group but rejected as ill-mannered by most well bred members of the other. Because deep down we know that in accordance with our national and Judaeo-Christian principles we should be one people, we are reluctant to admit that this divergence exists.

But the undeniable fact is that only now are we beginning to move toward our goal of oneness. We merely increase confusion if we allow ourselves to act on an assumption that already we are one people. The lesser of evils, I fear, is to concede that segregation has made us a nation within a nation, a people within a people.

Certainly we understand each other no better, and perhaps less well, than we understand European nations. Yet many members of each group tend to *think* they understand the other, and thus instead of trying to learn, they make judgments based on misinformation.

Among nations, divergent customs are taken for granted. When we visit another country, we expect to find many differences in practice; some will seem merely strange to us, others will be quite objectionable. Unless we are fools, we will not take any of these personally. We will know that these practices point only to the differences in customs of that people as compared to ours; they are not practices aimed at treating us differently from their own people. Much in the conduct of whites (though, of course, not all) that wounds and angers Negroes is this kind of practice, not an act personally directed toward the Negro.

THE ASSUMPTION THAT ALL IS PERSONAL

In crossing the border between colored and white America, we must not assume that only skin color, racial prejudice, and economic status will be different in those we meet. If we do, many innocent customs will appear to be acts of discrimination, and great injustice will be done persons who seek only to be our friends.

A Negro who enters an integrated situation and interprets everything as personal, expects indignities and snubs, watches for them and reacts to them, will end up inviting and multiplying very real ones. In addition, he will be imagining some which, in fact, are not there.

Bruised white acquaintances on the receiving end of his reactions may well not return for more of the same. Their avoidance of him will then be interpreted by him as racial rejection—and the vicious circle will go round and round.

Young whites tell me—sometimes tearfully—of overtures they made in heartfelt friendliness, which were rejected by Negroes with sullenness or even with sharp retorts. Often I can point out, as I tried to do in Part One, that the white all unaware has blundered. But it can also be the Negro who blunders. In this part I am trying to explain how and why.

3

DIVERGENT CUSTOMS

Attorney Joe Mills's office was closed for the weekend, but when May Evaston telephoned that she needed data in his files for a speech she must give Sunday, he offered to return to the office with her.

"But my wife has the car," he said. "Do you mind scooping me up on your way down?"

When May pulled to the curb in front of Joe's house, he was not to be seen; so she tooted softly. Jack-in-box style, his door flew open and out he catapulted, smacking it shut behind him. He strode down the walk to the car.

"It wouldn't do," he snapped, "for a black lawyer to sit beside a white lady! I'll get in back."

"What on earth has struck you?" May gasped.

"You have! And I had hoped you were one white person who didn't see me as 'a little darky trotting out of his shack totin' his Mammy's wash that she done so nice for de white fokes'!"

May stared. "I haven't the slightest idea what you're talking about, Joe Mills."

"Look," he said, "I've lived forty-nine years, and this is the first time I've *ever* had *any*one sit in a car and toot for me to come trotting!"

May started to laugh, then her shoulders sagged.

"Oh, *that!*" she said wearily. "Listen, Joe: in nearly *sixty* years *I've* never called for a man with*out* tooting if he wasn't outside waiting—as he should be. You're so scared of being short-changed on respect by some white person that you forget all about the courtesy due a woman by a man. How do you think your white friends feel, having to remember every second that you are a Negro or we give offense!"

They glared at each other for a moment, then Joe chuckled and got in beside her. "Okay, okay," he said, "I'll never argue with a lady who isn't my wife."

RACE CONSCIOUSNESS IN NEGROES

Incidents like this happen north, south, east, and west. From many examples I chose this one because May's complaint summarizes how most whites feel in such cases. Racial thinking in Negro friends is as shocking to integrated whites as it is to Negroes when they meet it in white friends. But it occurs to few Negroes that they are often more guilty of racial thinking than the white acquaintances they accuse.

Many Negroes do not know (though they often think they do) how whites behave toward one another; and just when a white has completely forgotten that he is dealing with a colored person, his Negro friend often jars him into race consciousness by accusations of "special treatment."

However, May's accusation that race consciousness blinded Joe to an obvious courtesy due a woman may have been unjust. Many differences in etiquette have developed on the two sides of the segregation wall, and one of them is that in some communities middle-aged and older Negroes tend to show much less deference to women than do whites of the same generations—though this contrast is not true of all communities, and it is almost always absent among younger people.

The reason for the difference may be that owing to the economic need for Negro American women to be bread-winners, they have all along been on a more equal footing with men, a relation white women have not had until quite recently. Negro women were thus deprived of some of the gallantry which stems from a belief that women are dependent on male protection.

The point is that in the white community of May's particular town no gentleman of her generation would have dreamed of behaving as Joe did. In Joe's community, on the other hand, gentlemen were not expected to wait outside for the lady coming for them, but to watch for her and come out when they saw her. And the lady, knowing that the man would soon appear, was expected to wait in decent silence.

But despite Joe's assertion that his being tooted for was a new experience, it did not occur to May that his misinterpretation was rooted in the different social practice of his group, and that even had she been colored, he would have thought her tooting rude.

This little incident is typical of the deadlock which often develops between Negro and Caucasian acquaintances—a racial tug-of-war almost—in which each sees himself as blameless and the other as race conscious, simply because neither is aware that in each group there are different sets of customs and a different code of manners. Joe, being the smarter of the two friends in this particular case, was the first to grasp what was really causing the misunderstanding, and to surrender.

MORE FORMALITY IN THE MINORITY

In most, if not all, areas where little or no mingling exists between the races, Negro citizens tend to be more formal with each other than do most white Americans today. This is noticeable at meetings of all kinds—social, church, civil rights, and club—but especially at business sessions of organizations where *Robert's Rules of Order* is generally more often invoked and strictly followed than at similar meetings among whites.

I know of no misunderstandings (though there may be some) which arise as a result of this tendency of Negro citizens to do things "decently and in order." I mention it here only because it so often is commented upon by whites who visit such meetings.

Unfortunately, the same cannot be said of many other practices. One in particular, which stems from a similar stress on formality, constantly causes friction and misinterpretation. This is the Negro's more frequent use within his own group of the courtesy titles Mr., Mrs., and Miss.

When whites of equal status meet in a relaxed situation and on common ground, they often call each other by their first names practically from the moment of introduction. In speaking of persons whom they know, even if the one they address does not know the particular persons, whites commonly say "Fred Carter" and "Milly Jones," rather than "Rev. Carter" and "Mrs. Jones."

In consequence, if a white is acting unself-consciously among colored acquaintances, he may address or refer to them by their first names much sooner than would a Negro. He will then be suspected of being the worst type of segregationist, unwilling even to extend this simple form of respect to Negroes.

On the other hand, when he learns better than that, he almost always offends in the opposite way. I continually hear from slightly integrated Negroes the complaint that whites discriminate by clinging to courtesy titles longer with Negroes than with whites.

THE INCONSISTENCY CONFUSES WHITES

Thus attacked from both sides, newly integrated whites often feel that no matter how hard they try, they cannot strike a note which rings true in the other group. Moving in colored society becomes for them an anxious struggle to balance themselves on a tightrope that sways first one way, then the other.

In the white group it is assumed that anyone wishing to be addressed by his first name will let the name be known early in the relationship. Once a habit is formed of addressing a person in a certain way, it is hard to change. But many Negroes appear to whites to make a point of keeping their first names a secret.

In addition to addressing and referring to each other by surnames, they commonly use only initials on letterheads and in telephone listings, even in signatures. Often the only way a white can learn a Negro's full name is by asking him or a close friend for it point blank. Confronted with a similar situation in his own group, a white would know that the person wanted to be addressed only formally.

Although I receive a flood of mail, I think I have not in my life got more than a score or so of letters from whites who sign themselves, "Mrs. Esther Smith" or "Mrs. Thomas J. Smith." They usually write "Esther Smith," then under it, "(Mrs. Thomas J. Smith)." But more than half my letters from Negroes are signed with courtesy titles prefixed.

Last year I saw a petition, copies of which had been circulated in both communities of a segregated town. In the white community even physicians signed without title, simply adding M.D. after their names. But in the colored community all women used titles without a single exception, and many men, even, signed with "Mr." To a white this seems a resounding demand that the title be used.

All the clues indicate to a white that Negroes wish no familiarities from him. Naturally, he responds by offering none. Colored Americans, no doubt, resorted to this practice not only in reaction against, but also for the purpose of stamping out, the insulting white habit (still common in the South) of withholding courtesy titles altogether from Negroes. The aim was sound, the method effective; and friendly whites take the very forthright and constantly reiterated hint.

After all this group-advertising to the contrary, if you want individual whites to address you informally, as they do each other, you have no recourse but to request it flatly and early—before the habit of addressing you formally is fixed.

NEGROES ARE CONFUSED TOO

Recently a middle-aged faculty wife told me of an experience with a Negro student. After chatting with him on several occasions, she dropped the "Mr." when addressing him, as she would with any student. But his reaction was unlike any other she had encountered: in reply he immediately dropped the "Mrs."

Because of her age and position, the inappropriateness of his act was startling, but since he was not a man of poor judgment in general, it seemed unlikely that he would have done such a thing had she been a member of his own group.

Did he imagine that her move really invited a similar one on his part? Did he think she was reacting as a white woman addressing a Negro, thus justifying this time-honored form of rebuke? We cannot know. But we do know that in her next sentence she returned to the "Mr."—as she would in like circumstances with any student—only later to learn that he thought this proof that she "wasn't ready to have Negroes address her in a friendly style."

The incident is typical, especially among younger Negroes, of confusion often created by mere knowledge of the existence of a color line. This young man would have known precisely how to behave with a colored faculty wife, but it did not occur to him that in this situation nothing was different except the lady's skin.

Many such blunders occur. And why not? On the one hand, there are customs which may unexpectedly differ, and on the other, there are people who unexpectedly may be just the same.

4

MORE STEREOTYPES

Jack Chandler and Kent Bannister were both in their thirties, both in the insurance business, both deeply concerned with the integration issue, and both enjoying their first intergroup friendship. Jack had never known anyone with whom he was so congenial as with Kent, and he felt very superior to persons who complained of the mistrust of colored acquaintances.

But slowly, mysteriously, the friendship began to fall apart. Kent withdrew into a cool shell of formality. Searching his soul for an explanation, Jack found none and at last asked flatly:

"Kent, have I done something you don't like? You don't seem the same."

"The same as what?"

"As you were at first. Why has our friendship soured?"

"What friendship?"

Jack was silent a moment. "To me it was a friendship. I never felt closer to any friend."

"You mean, any *colored* friend."

"Darn it, no! What kind of a crack is that?"

"I know how white friends talk together," Kent said. "*We* never talk about anything but integration and business."

"What's wrong with that? They're the things we're most interested in. That's why it's fun being with you—we have the same work and the same hobby."

Kent said nothing. Finally Jack asked, "You don't mean we should talk about women, do you? I happen to be in love with my wife."

Kent winced. "I know you've tried, Jack. But there's not much to build on when it just doesn't occur to you that I could talk about anything but business and integration—unless, of course, sex! Music, art, literature, philosophy, you think aren't discussable with a Negro."

"Are you serious? I haven't kicked that intellectual stuff around since college bull sessions."

Kent's tone was skeptical: "You mean you don't discuss books, paintings, and so on with your friends? I do with mine."

"Heck, no! I'm too busy to keep up with all that. Let the long hairs have it."

THE STEREOTYPE OF CULTURED WHITES

Negroes who have attended predominantly white colleges are especially prone to imagine that whites conduct rarified conversations among themselves. Most people talk about what they are doing; so college students engaged in acquiring a broad cultural base naturally talk about their studies. Colored Americans, whose only social contact with whites has been during this period of learning, often confuse the situation with the people and assume that all educated whites talk like college students.

Educated Negroes (perhaps in a pendulum swing away from oppression-induced ignorance) by and large tend to be more culture-minded than whites in comparable circumstances. Unless a white happens to have a culture-oriented hobby or career, his general level of conversation probably is such that colored friends are almost sure to think he is "talking down."

With educated Negro women, I hardly dare mention topics that are my favorites with white women—how with less time one can be a better homemaker, how with less money have better meals, how to be more companionable with one's family, and so on. To me these are the fascinating problems which most married women share and can help each other with. Yet if I turn to them with a colored friend, she usually concludes (and gently lets me know) that I am being condescending.

When I am truly congenial with someone, 80 per cent of my conversation revolves around integration or religion. But these subjects, above all, are construed by colored acquaintances as chosen for their special benefit.

My avoidance of literature as a topic always is misinterpreted. The fact is that I know embarrassingly little about it. I write, not because of any literary talent or interest in literature, but because I have a lot I want to say. Although I once was a portrait painter, I painted—knowing no more about art than I do about literature—simply to convey ideas I wanted to express. As for music, I am tone deaf.

I feel quite as if an assailant has his foot on my neck if someone tries to steer me into discussing the arts or anything else that an educated person ought to know. I confess here because it seldom occurs to Negroes that a white may avoid discussing cultural topics with them through feelings of inferiority rather than of superiority.

THE STEREOTYPE OF CAUCASIAN INTELLIGENCE

While conscious of the white assumption that Caucasians are smarter, Negroes are less aware that they themselves operate on this false premise. Let us recall here that the final experts on race, the anthropologists, unanimously affirm that there is no acceptable evidence that Negroes are, in innate mental ability, inferior to Caucasians. The colored man has simply succumbed to the white man's self-acclaim. However, a white can hardly cross the color line without being conscious that Negroes are assuming him to be brighter than whites do.

This is far from an unmixed blessing. When I first moved out of the white race into the human race, I constantly was tormented by the Negro's supposition that my knowledge and intelligence were great and, therefore, that every idiot's blunder I made was calculated and intentional. Actually I had been accustomed to people assuming that I was well meaning but dumb when I pulled a boner. The shock of the reverse interpretation was nearly unbearable.

Intelligent modern Negroes usually are experts on the evils of segregation, and since we all tend to assume that others know facts that are overfamiliar to us, Negroes naturally believe whites understand the content of segregation much better than they, the whites, actually do. And this misconception is magnified to serious proportions by the stereotype of whites as being brilliant and well informed.

The American Negro takes it for granted that whites know and evaluate with absolute clarity the handicaps and suffering which segregation inflicts on the minority. He, therefore, concludes that they must be unspeakably morally corrupt.

THE INCREDIBILITY OF WHITE IGNORANCE

Recently one of our most brilliant and perceptive Negro leaders, after meeting with a committee of well-known white moderates, exclaimed that he was "surprised and unbelieving" when he saw how little they knew about the modern Negro's situation and his attitudes toward it. Shortly thereafter, a distinguished Negro psychologist cried out that he was "shocked, appalled" when confronted by this same ignorance in the nation's political leaders.

These statements from such men point forcefully to the white man's shocking lack of knowledge about people with whom he daily deals. They also point to something else.

It happens that the chief key to the white American's attitudes and behavior in regard to integration—a key without which he cannot possibly be understood—is his abysmal ignorance of what transpires, both within and without, in the lives of his darker brothers. Failure to use this key means that the white man's conduct in regard to civil rights cannot be interpreted with any comprehension whatever.

So when Negroes express surprise at the Caucasian's ignorance of the basic facts of the integration issue, it actually means that in their negotiations with the white man Negroes have lacked the essential key for success in that effort.

WE KNOW THE WHITE MAN

Understandably weary of the decrepit white claim so often heard in the South, "We know the Negro," many colored citizens are prone to say that while this is not true, the reverse is— *the Negro knows the white*. After fourteen years of struggling with stereotypes and misinterpretations applied to me because I am white, I could not agree less.

When I first began to realize how wrong segregation is, I went from one Negro to another asking questions—and learning almost nothing. They assumed I knew all the elementary facts about the effect of segregation on a minority and, therefore, devoted themselves entirely to pointing out how uneconomical, undemocratic, and un-Christian it is to humiliate and handicap fellow citizens and to deny to others freedoms that one claims for oneself.

Now I had always, long before I began to doubt the rightness of segregation, been ready to concede all that. What I did not understand was how segregation could humiliate, handicap, and deny freedoms to anyone. Without a single exception, Negroes assumed that it was moral enlightenment that I needed, when what I really needed was an elementary school, even a kindergarten, education in the facts of segregation.

I had seen the segregation wall only from the outside—the free side. I had no information that helped me to understand that on the other side it was a prison wall. Many whites sincerely ask themselves and others the question, "If we don't find it a handicap to stay with our kind, why do Negroes think it a handicap to stay with theirs?" Yet Negroes find it impossible to believe that we can escape knowing that segregation is a prison. "It's right before your eyes," they insist. "How can you help seeing it?"

The answer is that segregation has done an even better job of separating us than we realize. White people are not taught anything about it in their schools. They cannot learn about it from their friends, for they do not know about it either.

We see no Negro newspapers, and white papers seldom say anything that will help an uninformed person understand why the minority group finds segregation insupportable when the majority group does not. News stories report only what people do and say, not why they do and say it.

Most public protests by Negro leaders make not one bit of sense to the average white because he does not know what lies behind them. The whole Negro revolution looks one way if you realize that colored Americans are trying to escape from a situation that any normal person would abhor, seeking only to obtain what every American is entitled to. It looks a very different way if you imagine, as many whites do, that the Negro wants to invade white territory for no better reason than that it is white. Whites, remember, are segregated too, and they have little information which helps them realize that the Negro's experience of segregation is entirely different from their own.

NO HELP FROM NEGROES

When a white person begins to wonder about segregation and tries to learn about it, the chances are that he will merely get more misinformation and become further confused—even if he turns to Negroes themselves for help.

Most Negroes so mistrust whites that when a white starts asking about segregation, they think he is pulling some kind of trick. They usually avoid a direct answer and reply so vaguely that the questioner learns nothing. Outside the South, Negroes may reply sarcastically; in the South, they may tell him what they think he wants to hear: that they like segregation just fine! The more questions he asks, the more suspicious they usually are, for they cannot believe that he does not already know the answers.

But he really does not. All the miserable, everyday inconveniences and frustration which are overfamiliar to colored Americans were absolutely new to me in 1950, and still—despite all that has been written recently on the subject—are unknown to most whites, North and South. Personal involvement—personal relationships with those who have suffered segregation—is needed to penetrate this ignorance.

I do not mean that if everyone were to recognize segregation to be a prison for colored Americans, all white persons would immediately want them freed. But I do mean that if everyone did know this, there would be a noticeable change in the climate of opinion, especially in the South where misinformation is at its worst.

I do mean that we would at once gain a helpful number of influential supporters from among sincerely religious people who now see no conflict—just as I once did—between their faith and the practice of segregation. This means that on the civil rights front *there is a pressing need for Negroes who will act as ambassadors and missionaries to the white group.*

5

THE GANGSTER IN
THE HAUNTED HOUSE

In Chapter 9, Part One, the intermarriage issue was likened to a haunted house, and we strove to lay ghosts and reduce the fright-mask's power. But lurking still is a brutal gangster, and until jailed, he will permit no peace.

Let me here anticipate speculation by nakedly stating my own views. When I am asked, "Would you want your daughter to marry a Negro?" my answer is, "Yes—under some conditions."

What conditions? Chiefly, under the condition that the situation would be one where my personal feelings regarding intermarriage are the only factor to be considered. I believe that an individual's free choice of his mate is an inalienable right, that laws restricting this choice are unconstitutional, and that intermarriage is morally right. I hope for the gangster's capture and for the day when what is now a haunted house for many will be a happy home for all.

While the killer roams free, I claim no freedom from fear. But I hope, and believe, that if ever I meet him face to face, I will not run away.

THE MINORITY'S THREE QUESTIONS

The colored man's bewilderment at the white man's fears of intermarriage is expressed in three main questions: (1) Why do whites think we want to marry them? (2) Why do they feel they would have to let us if we did want to? (3) Why does the prospect frighten them so?

I shall not review the familiar answers to these perennial questions, not because I reject those answers but because it seems better to offer new light than to point out lamps already lit. The purpose of this book, remember, is to help Negroes and whites understand each other. My answers are oriented toward that purpose and are meant neither to accuse nor to defend.

THE FIRST QUESTION

One reason for the assumption that Negroes want to marry whites is, quite simply, that whites are in a top-dog situation. Any persons—irrespective of color—who have cornered economic or social advantages tend to feel that they are marital targets for the less fortunate. Marrying into a higher income or prestige bracket is a well-known (and relatively easy) means of bettering one's circumstances. People in advantageous positions naturally suspect others of wanting to marry them.

Some opponents of integration also point out that groups with high incomes, prestige, or political power always have romantic appeal for groups having less advantages, quite apart from the desire to reap material benefits. The less privileged, it is said, seek mates, as a matter of course, from the privileged groups.

Still another reason for the assumption that Negroes desire intermarriage goes back to ignorance of the content of segregation. Not understanding what colored Americans are running away from in segregation, most white Americans are baffled by the intensity of their drive toward integration. The vehemence seems disproportionate to the need. Thus the sex drive (always a standard explanation for much of man's otherwise inexplicable behavior) offers a handy solution to the mystery of the passionate urgency of integration demands.

These three indisputable facts—the fact that it is expedient to marry into a more advantaged group; that such a group has romantic appeal; and that sex is a common motivation—when taken together make it a perfectly rational, though erroneous, conclusion that intermarriage is a primary Negro goal. But let me again stress that this explanation is in *addition* to, not instead of, the familiar ones which point to neuroses, guilt feelings, and racial stereotypes as the roots of this conclusion.

Neuroses, guilt feelings, and stereotypes certainly are among its roots. However, we all tend to exaggerate their role in the thinking of our enemies—and our exaggeration handicaps us. As exponents of nonviolence, we well know that any final triumph over enemies comes about by making them friends. This is not done by overstressing inhuman, unreasonable aspects of their thinking or by ignoring aspects that are fully human and understandable.

THE SECOND QUESTION

"If their daughter doesn't want to marry a Negro, she can just say, 'No.' " This has become a classic exposition of the irrationality of intermarriage fears. Irrational though many of these fears certainly are, they are probably no more so than any other extreme fear. Any extreme fear usually takes leave of reality and, like cancer, leads a life of its own.

A man afraid of dogs views with suspicion obviously lethargic, toothless old hounds. A woman afraid of burglars witlessly expects them nightly, even if there is nothing to steal. So to say that the white's intermarriage fears are irrational, really is only to say that they are intense. But why are they so intense?

THE THIRD QUESTION

The inquiry "Why are whites so afraid?" often is coupled with the question "Are all whites neurotic?" The answer, of course, is that a lot of them are, just as a lot of Negroes are. Neuroses certainly account for much of the fear of miscegenation. So do racial "apparitions" and the "Halloween mask" discussed in Chapter 9, Part One. Misinformation takes its toll, too. A nationwide survey made in 1957, by the National Opinion Research Center of Chicago, revealed that a sizeable minority of whites still mistakenly believed in the basic biological inferiority of Negroes—a belief that naturally heightens intermarriage fear.

Within the general question "Why are whites afraid?" I think two more specific questions are implied: "Why are even white liberals afraid?" and "Why is marrying 'a Negro' spoken of as though it doesn't matter what kind of person he is?"

The answer to both questions is that there are realistic, practical reasons (as well as the apparitional and subjective ones reviewed in Chapter 9) for a white to fear the marriage of a relative to a Negro—any Negro—regardless of his personal superiority, wealth, or position of importance in world affairs. Depending on the degree of enlightenment and liberality of the individual, considerations that are quite realistic are always *a* chief factor or *the* chief factor or the *only* factor in his intermarriage fears.

THE GANGSTER

Since there is a real, powerful, ruthless, armed-to-the-teeth, and utterly destructive gangster in the haunted house of intermarriage fears, no normal parent—it makes no difference how dedicated he may be to the brotherhood of man—can fail to quake when confronted with this peril.

This gangster is the nationwide social climate in regard to intermarriage. The climate, please note, is quite chilly (in practice if not in principle) even in the Negro group. It is subzero in the white group.

There is no moral justification for the existence of such a climate. But this merely parallels the fact that there is none for the existence of gangsters, either. It does not change the sad circumstances that both gangsters and harsh opinion exist and that both are able—eager!—to maim and destroy anyone who challenges them.

If you are white and your daughter (son, brother, or sister) marries a Negro, you can reasonably expect that all your social relationships will be affected in some way. And if your family, or the groom's, has any claim to distinction, you can be sure that the machine-gun fire of vicious publicity will cut you down. In this respect, you will be better off if he is obscure than if he is a Ralph Bunche. You can expect rivals to laugh, friends to pity, neighbors to hope you will move away; you can perhaps even expect adverse economic repercussions to follow.

The relatives of the person who marries a Negro will suffer most—which may be why whites remain unimpressed by the classic answer, "She can just say no." The girl will gain the one she loves and therefore may not wish to say no, but her relatives will gain nothing and lose much.

Moreover, in intergroup marriage, realistic white parents— even if they are personally crusading for the elimination of every barrier, including the gangster—cannot, while the gangster lies in wait, help feeling fear for the welfare of their child. Even if the young couple are made for each other, so that slights and pressures serve more as a challenge than a threat to their love, a stony path awaits the white wife (or husband) of a Negro:

She will be subject to all the handicaps, frustrations, and wounds that prejudice inflicts on Negroes, but she will lack the fellowship of being an accepted part of their group. She will be an outsider to her own group, but not an insider to her husband's.

And what parent would not ache at the thought of grand-children born with so many strikes against them?

Some of these dangers confront Negroes also, and colored parents, too, fear intermarriage. Minority endorsement of it is given more in principle than in practice. The white's much greater fear, though it often is rooted in prejudice, sometimes stems entirely from two factors which provide sufficient cause:

First, a white girl who marries a Negro has to offer herself deliberately and by choice as a target for discrimination. Her husband already is—all his life has been—discriminated against, while in marrying him, she marries discrimination.

Second, disapproval of mixed marriages among Negroes, while it can be unpleasant, is not comparable to the frozen ostracism or frenzied fury met by parents and "culprit" among whites.

FOUR BASIC FEARS

In this chapter, just as in Chapter 9, Part One, we have striven to untangle the snarl of fact and fiction, reason and irrationality, prudence and panic, that surround the intermarriage issue. We have discovered four primary fears, two of which we have discussed at length. The first is one we all share, fear of the gangster of public opinion. The second is the prejudiced white's fear that biological perils lie in miscegenation. This, as we pointed out, is a mere apparition.

The third, not yet discussed, is the white liberal's fear of losing minority friends if he admits his terror of the gangster. This situation of the white liberal is grave. Having largely broken with his own group to stand with Negroes, he cannot endure loss of fellowship with Negroes, too.

The fourth is the Negro's fear that Caucasian dread of intermarriage means simply a complete and final rejection of Negroes, including himself, on the part of the Caucasian. In very prejudiced persons, racial rejection does play a leading role. But even with them, the gangster gets co-star billing. And I suspect that with most whites the gangster plays the lead.

With any white who firmly holds out his hand to you, in the South at least, you may be sure the gangster is the *only* factor. By offering you his hand, he is saying, "We should be together." Be certain he means it, for in taking your hand he places you in the balance against all the rest of his world. He has much to lose and, be assured, he will lose it.

He has only your friendship to gain but for reasons we shall review in the final chapter, you are worth all losses if indeed he gains you. Your mistrust, however, cuts deep. It would mean much to him if you would try to grasp the sense of helpless isolation that overtakes a white who must move against the gigantic fears and granite opinion of his group on the intermarriage issue.

Much that he most values is subject to destruction. There is no one to turn to—unless to you. There is refuge nowhere. He has no hiding place. He must crouch alone in the haunted house, the gangster's switchblade at his throat.

6

BULLDOGS FOR BROTHERHOOD

"When I drive a few blocks into the Negro community, a nightmare takes hold of me. I seem to be in a field of snakes with their tails rattling.

"All my life people have accepted me at face value. Nobody has ever seemed to doubt that my motives or intentions were what I claimed. Whenever I have been friendly, I've made friends; always when I said something, it was believed.

"But only a few blocks away, all that is changed. When I'm friendly, Negroes *wonder why!* Nothing I say is understood just as I mean it. Every word is twisted into a new shape. Suspicion, anger, mysterious sullenness appear suddenly on faces as I stand there every inch sincere, every inch concerned, seeking only to understand and to be understood. Never am I accepted for what I am.

"I'm always on the witness stand when I talk to a Negro; always being prosecuted for something I didn't do—or, at least, didn't purposely do. Everyone looks at me with the eyes of a prosecutor!"

This letter is from a young white Northerner who has just fully awakened to the fact of inequality and wants to work for a better America. The question is, Can he endure his first experiences of "brotherhood" long enough to learn what lies behind them?

PROSECUTED FOR FRIENDSHIP

If you think he exaggerates his predicament, I assure you that he does not. His experience is common—though not inevitable—for whites who attempt the steep climb to genuine intergroup fellowship.

Moreover, although the most ruthless prosecutions usually come at the outset (just when the accused may most easily be discouraged), integrated whites can never hope to put these ordeals entirely behind them. No law protects them, as it does the criminal, from being tried over and over for the same offense.

Although the white's crime may exist only in the minds of his accusers, although the only tangible evidence against him may be his white skin, nevertheless month after month, year after year, each new Negro acquaintance automatically turns prosecutor and thrusts him on the witness stand. Weary, increasingly bruised, the accused goes through it all again—again—again.

Liberal whites are met with these ordeals, please note, not merely in spite of not having personally deserved them but actually *because* they have not. Judy, you recall, asked students to dinner who had never entered a white home. The students did not prosecute the many people who had not invited them to a meal. They prosecuted Judy.

It is precisely because these whites make overtures of friendship to Negroes, precisely because they break away from their own group to seek remedies for injustice done their darker brothers, that the glaring spotlight of suspicion focuses on them. Negroes are at ease with their enemies. It is their supporters whom they suspect, misinterpret, accuse.

SPECIAL TREATMENT FOR WHITES

Colored young people today rightly have been taught that kowtowing to whites, currying favor by insincerities, or playing Uncle Tom to the "master race" is contemptible. No one should be cajoled for any ulterior reason, and especially not merely because his skin is white. A Negro must, for the integrity of his own soul, ignore the white man's unnatural power and treat him as he would any other man.

But I have news for many who think they already do this: *I would endure from no white person,* and I suspect *you would endure from no Negro,* the suspicion, rudeness and insulting misinterpretation to which one Negro after another has subjected me as I fought beside him for freedom and equality for all.

UNNATURAL RELATIONSHIP

Although it is far from true of all colored Americans, nevertheless many of them do easily slip into the groove of thinking it their right—their duty, even—to suspect, test and rebuke any friendly white until his sincerity is proven to their personal satisfaction. They seem to be totally unaware of the effect of such treatment on their victim.

These painful experiences are not normally encountered in the course of a friendship. An attractive, friendly white person may have never before in his life, until he met you, encountered suspicion, "tests," or rebukes for offenses he had not intended. Can he, then, help comparing how you make him feel with how other friends make him feel?

If you could see how you look in this comparison, you might get a shock. A relationship with a Negro often is so distorted, so unnatural, because of his suspicions and resentments that only a white who is what I call a bulldog-for-brotherhood will continue to subject himself to it.

Yet a friend who seeks you out only because you are a

Negro and he is a bulldog-for-brotherhood is not the kind of friend you want, is he? There is little satisfaction in being liked only by those who, on principle, will put up with anything. Half the joy in being liked is the proof it offers that we are likable.

You naturally want to be sought after for the same reasons that any friend is sought after. What are those reasons? Most of us choose friends who give us a sense of shared fellowship, mutual exchange of thought and feeling, and success in our efforts to be good company. In short, we feel secure and pleased with ourselves when we are with them. If someone makes us feel the opposite, we do not seek his company for its own sake.

To be sought for the joy of being with him, a person's companionship must be enjoyable. Few things are less enjoyable than the feeling that we are constantly saying and doing the wrong thing, that we are forever treading on someone's sore toe, that we are continually being wondered about, suspected, and judged.

Of course, to express to a white your anger and suspicion is healthier than to suppress these feelings through fear. Only a score of years ago, few Negroes would have *dared* behave as many do now. With this sign of progress the white crusader for equality salves his wounds.

NO REGRETS FOR INJUSTICE

"Do you know," a white integrationist recently remarked to me, "that of all the times I've been cross-questioned, frozen, or chided by colored friends for things I wasn't guilty of, not one has ever expressed regret later for torturing me with unjust suspicions?"

I did know.

"I think they take suspecting whites so for granted," I said, "that it hardly occurs to them that we mightn't take it for granted, too. But aren't you used to it by now?"

"How can you get used to being mistrusted by a friend? I know only one cure for such suffering, and that's to stop thinking of anyone as a friend. I hope I never have that cure."

I fear I must agree. Each time I am doubted, I still feel most of the incredulity I felt the first time it happened. I still am frustrated at being misunderstood, still recoil from the sting of hostility, still ache at being weighed in the balance for rejection.

Even if he has experienced it before, a straight thinking person can hardly twist his thoughts into expecting such an unnatural course of events as being prosecuted for friendliness. Indeed, to accept it, to become resigned to it, would almost be to let one's human sensibilities drain off through one's wounds.

I have been fully acquitted in every trial. At least, I have been told so by my judges. Yet instead of the welcome words, "I'm sorry I doubted you; I should have known," my accusers offer only assurances that I have emerged from the trial triumphant. *Triumphant?* I have convinced them of my sincerity, they say in tones implying that I have done well and they are glad to admit it. I have made the grade; they believe me now! (Until the next time, of course.)

NO CONQUEST THROUGH CRUSADERS

White warriors on the civil rights front are thus forced to expend in these trials and retrials energy that could be far better spent in the fight for equality. But what really matters here is that these patterns of behavior which we encounter in some Negroes must be met by average whites who, though goodwilled, lack the sense of total dedication to brotherhood.

We bulldogs-for-brotherhood, we crusaders, can take these trials. But there can be little success for our mutual endeavors if the brotherhood we are trying to build can rest only on a foundation of bulldogs-for-brotherhood and crusaders.

Average friendly whites must be brought into intergroup

fellowship else we will not, cannot, move far toward the brotherhood of man. Yet as things now stand, I doubt if any except the bulldog can survive more than a few months on the brotherhood front.

True, in Part One I urged whites to seek out an angry, even hostile teacher, as though a figurative punch in the jaw were just what we all need. That is because Part One is addressed primarily to bulldogs—to the already convinced, whose consciences are fully awake and who ache to make amends. A stiff punch for them may well be an eye-opener. For the average good-willed white, the same punch may result in a K.O.

There are myriads of whites in this land who have oppressed Negroes in pure ignorance of what they did. As colored citizens continue to cry out against injustice, these whites begin first to see the truth, then to take their earliest stumbling steps toward undoing the evil. If they meet with ill-treatment from those whose cause they wish to support, anger and hatred may well replace the old thoughtlessness and ignorance. In this connection, the technique for breaking stereotypes, which was suggested at the end of Part One, will serve you well.

As we move toward integrated situations, whether the final result will be one of enmity or fellowship rests in the hands of those of us who first scale the wall. The future of America itself hangs on our ability to meet each person as an individual human being.

It hangs on our ability to forget that he is one color, we another; on our ability to remember that we all—old and young, stupid and bright, bad and good—are never any more than confused and stumbling children, or any less than children of God.

PART THREE:

FOR
ALL
OF US

FOR ALL OF US

In this book we have reviewed many obstacles to intergroup friendship. For some the cumulative effect may be one of discouragement. But just as a manual on machine repair does not intend to imply that the machinery will always be out of order, neither does this book mean to imply that white and colored friends are always having trouble.

Actually, the book's very existence is proof of progress. Psychological barriers to pleasant relationships are of little interest to readers (or publishers) until the desire for such relationships has become fairly widespread. Obstacles to understanding have been reviewed here precisely because, were they removed, genuine fellowship could result.

Moreover, once they become real friends, Negroes and whites often give each other more wholehearted acceptance than do most friends of one's own group. The obstacles we have been discussing are met chiefly in the early stages of the relationship.

PERSONAL REWARDS

Despite the shocks, disappointments, and wounds that the budding fellowship between whites and Negroes now often includes, the experience is a deeply rewarding one. In it is a beauty, richness, and fullness of satisfaction seldom found in other earthly relationships.

A sense of triumph results—perhaps from the sheer magnitude of the task. When one finally succeeds in bridging the canyon that separates him from a friend of another color, something exciting is proven about himself, his species, and the world. The friendship proves that the nobler side of man has dominion over the forces that divide and retard humanity. Fighting his way upward to stand beside his brother, a man knows that he wins a victory for life itself—for integration—against the forces of disintegration which are death.

Whites and Negroes who achieve this meeting of minds commonly experience an expansion of vision, as though they surveyed their world from a height. A sense of wholeness, too, is felt when the two largest segments of American humanity unite and face the world as one.

The relationship itself between a Negro and white often begins on a higher level than ordinary friendships. Conflicts, we know, tend to show themselves at the more egotistical levels of consciousness. Therefore, in intergroup relationships our spirits are forced upward to realms of broad human values, creative insights, and universal principles.

To speak specifically for certain Southerners, we experience genuine joy when we see the fulfillment of the promises that life seemed to make long ago. As children, white and colored Southerners often knew and loved each other. As adults, laws and customs forced us apart, but for many of us this separation could not be the last word. Something deep in us denied it. Nostalgia for each other haunted our hearts and minds. The bond was still there—living, eternal, real. So, now, fellowship between us, even when fleeting and fraught with frustration and pain, affirms something that our hearts know is true.

UNIVERSAL REWARDS

Negro Americans are presently the best Americans. In them the nation's history is repeating itself. They feel and think as Jeffersonian Americans once felt and thought.

White Americans oppress Negroes much as the British oppressed our colonists, and their inner response is like that of the colonists.* They see the American vision of freedom and justice for all with a clarity not shared by our white citizens today.

The hope of America—perhaps her only hope—is in her minorities. They understand the American ideal much better than the white majority do. The modern Negro leader has the firm grip on American ideals which our founding fathers had, but which modern whites have lost.

Our Constitution was framed by people who suffered oppression much like that which Negro citizens now suffer. Only persons who have been denied freedom, equality, and human dignity can appreciate the value of our national charter with its affirmation of freedom, rights, and dignity to all.

Communism proclaims that it offers a full stomach and a measure of security to everyone, and it is spreading its philosophy with dedication and passion. We shall not win against it with the tepid concern for democratic freedoms that characterizes white Americans who have long taken them for granted.

But colored Americans thirst and hunger for the full realization of our chartered democracy. Their conviction has power and thrust. We need their help to awaken our nation to the reality of what our freedoms mean.

Our colored citizens must make friends among our white citizens. People learn more readily from friends than from strangers. Negro Americans have much to teach—white Ameri-

* By God's grace, however, their tactics have not been the same. Negro Americans are achieving by legal and other effective but undestructive means what white Americans achieved less nobly.

cans much to learn. Our largest minority must deliver and redeem our land. They must be leaven in the American lump, so that we all, in turn, can be leaven in the lump of the world.

THE SECRET OF FELLOWSHIP

Increasingly our colored citizens are standing for, acting out, the great American theme, "freedom and justice for all." But more! Leading Negro Christians are standing for, acting out, the great Christian theme, "Love your unlovable neighbor because God loves you."

All great thoughts have many times been spoken. Only when they are acted out, do they move into their inherent greatness. No man is great in himself. The brilliant, the forceful, are trivial when they merely flex their mental muscles. Men become great when they stand for a great cause or act out a great conviction.

Thus, colored Americans who move with their whole persons to seek, teach and materialize the valiant dormant ideals of our nation are the great Americans today. In them the soul of America vibrates with new life. In them often can be seen the passionate, compassionate love of God—which can redeem us all if white Americans, too, will act out their noblest insights and hopes.

In acting them out together, we will find the over-all answer to intergroup relations. For alienated brothers cannot be reclaimed except in the context of labor for a common cause. If we would reach, touch, know one another, we must work together for a purpose larger than ourselves, a purpose we all share.

The language of brotherly love is not a spoken language but one that must be acted out. We can never talk our way into hearts, minds and lives. We can best communicate with one another when we work in unison for freedom, justice and acceptance for all, seeking together a better community, nation and world.

APPENDIX

This is a list of the national offices of some of the well-known organizations whose primary concern is the destruction of discrimination and intergroup prejudice.* Send cards asking the location of their chapters nearest you.

American Friends Service Committee
Mr. Harold Evans, Chairman
160 North 15th St., Philadelphia 2, Pa.

Anti-Defamation League of B'nai B'rith
Mr. Benjamin R. Epstein, National Director
315 Lexington Ave., New York City 10016

Congress on Racial Equality
James Farmer, Director
38 Park Row, New York City 10038

* There are also many regional and state organizations with these matters as primary concerns, besides a large number that count these matters among their secondary concerns.

Episcopal Society for Cultural and Racial Unity
John Morris, Executive Director
5 Forsyth St., N.W., Atlanta 3, Ga.

National Association for the Advancement of Colored People
Roy Wilkins, Executive Secretary
20 West 40th Street, New York City 10018

National Catholic Conference for Interracial Justice
Mr. Mathew Ahmann, Executive Director
21 West Superior St., Chicago 10, Ill.

National Conference of Christians and Jews
Dr. Lewis Webster Jones, President
43 West 57th St., New York City 10019

National Council of Churches
Dr. R. H. Edwin Espy, General Secretary
475 Riverside Drive, New York City 10027

National Urban League
Whitney Young, Executive Director
14 East 48th St., New York City 10017

Southern Christian Leadership Conference
Martin Luther King, Director
334 Auburn Ave., N.E., Atlanta, Ga. 30303

Southern Regional Council, Inc.*
Leslie Dunbar, Executive Director
5 Forsyth St., N.W., Atlanta 3, Ga.

* A good source of literature and general information on the whole issue.

Student Nonviolent Coordinating Committee
John Lewis, Chairman
6 Raymond St., N.W., Atlanta 14, Ga.

Note: For information about the program of a national church write to the church's national headquarters; or to the Commission on Religion and Race, National Council of Churches, 475 Riverside Drive, New York City 10027.